TURNING POINTS

By Therese Harasymiw

AUSCHWITZ AND THE HOLOCAUST

Cavendish Square

New York

Published in 2022 by Cavendish Square Publishing, LLC
29 E. 21st Street, New York, NY 10010

First Edition

Website: cavendishsq.com

Portions of this work were originally authored by David Robson and published as *Auschwitz* (*World History*). All new material this edition authored by Therese Harasymiw.

All websites were available and accurate when this book was sent to press.

Library of Congress Cataloging-in-Publication Data

Names: Harasymiw, Therese, author.
Title: Auschwitz and the Holocaust / Therese Harasymiw.
Description: New York : Cavendish Square Publishing, [2022] | Series: Turning points | Includes bibliographical references and index.
Identifiers: LCCN 2021006164 | ISBN 9781502660817 (library binding) | ISBN 9781502660800 (paperback) | ISBN 9781502660824 (ebook)
Subjects: LCSH: Auschwitz (Concentration camp)–Juvenile literature. | World War, 1939-1945–Concentration camps–Juvenile literature. | Holocaust, Jewish (1939-1945)–Juvenile literature. | Jews–Persecutions–Europe–Juvenile literature.
Classification: LCC D805.5.A96 H36 2022 | DDC 940.53/1853862–dc23
LC record available at https://lccn.loc.gov/2021006164

Editor: Therese Shea
Copy Editor: Abby Young
Designer: Deanna Paternostro

CPSIA compliance information: Batch #CS22CSQ: For further information contact Cavendish Square Publishing LLC, New York, New York at 1-877-980-4450.

Printed in the United States of America

TABLE OF CONTENTS

INTRODUCTION

WHY WE MUST REMEMBER

Every year on January 27, people around the world gather to remember one of the most horrific events in human history—the Holocaust. International Holocaust Remembrance Day was created so people would never forget the systematic killing of 6 million Jewish people and millions of others under the rule of Nazi Germany before and during World War II.

In recent years, it has become more important than ever to continue to talk and learn about what happened during the Holocaust and what made such a tragedy possible. As time has passed and survivors of the Holocaust have died, the facts about this period in history are becoming lost to time. Although it is one of the defining events of the 20th century, a 2018 survey showed that more than 20 percent of American adults around the ages of 25 to 40 were not sure they had ever heard of the Holocaust.

As knowledge of the Holocaust has decreased, the kinds of hatred that fueled it have increased. Anti-Semitism—discrimination toward and hatred of Jewish people—is on the rise in many countries, including the United States. One of the most infamous examples of this was the "Unite the Right" rally that took place in Charlottesville, Virginia, in August 2017. Marchers chanted slogans

Nations around the world honor Holocaust Remembrance Day with services and memorials such as this one in Ukraine.

such as "Jews will not replace us!"[1] and raised their hands in Nazi salutes. What had seemed like a horrible part of history was suddenly front-page news once again.

Many people believe it is important to learn about the Holocaust, but it can be hard to discover the details of such a dark part of the past. Learning about the Holocaust brings up difficult questions about why so many people were able to ignore—or actively participate in—the mass murder of their fellow human beings. However, examining these difficult questions is necessary to build a better world. As the saying goes, those who do not learn from history are doomed to repeat it.

A Dictator Rises

A closer look at the Holocaust must begin with a closer look at the rise of the man who controlled Nazi Germany and everything that happened under its reign: Adolf Hitler. How could a man like Hitler rise to power? The answer is a combination of economic instability and fervent nationalism.

In October 1929, the stock market crashed in the United States, causing millions of people to lose all their money. Because no one had money to spend anymore, the economy fell into what became known as the Great Depression. People stopped buying goods, so factories stopped producing as much and had to fire many of their workers. With so many people out of work, the crisis got worse—not only in the United States but also in other countries around the world.

The German economy was especially vulnerable because the country was one of those that had lost World War I. After the fighting ended in 1918, it had to pay reparations, meaning that Germany was responsible for paying for damage the war had done to other countries. It owed $33 billion at the time, which would be more than $400 billion today. In addition to having massive debts to pay that made their economy even weaker than those of other struggling nations, the German people were still angry about the lands and power Germany had lost in the war.

Adolf Hitler joined a political party in 1919 called the German Workers' Party. It was renamed the National Socialist German Workers' Party, or the Nazi Party, in 1920. Hitler decided to run for president in 1932, appealing to people's anger and nationalism and declaring that he would make Germany a great nation, as it had been in the past. He lost the election but was appointed chancellor, a powerful political position.

As chancellor, Hitler abused his power. After a fire broke out in the Reichstag (German parliament building) in 1933, he blamed the Communist Party and stoked fears that members were planning a violent uprising in Germany. Capitalizing on national anxiety, Hitler and the German government were able to pass a decree that abolished many basic freedoms, including those of free speech and free press, and allowed authorities to arrest political opponents without cause.

Adolf Hitler became a popular figure because he knew how to manipulate people's anger. He did this by promising them a return to power and wealth and by blaming other people, especially the Jewish people, for the problems many Germans were facing.

When the German president died in 1934, the Nazis created a law that combined the positions of president and chancellor, making Hitler effectively dictator of Germany. The Nazis called their government the Third Reich. The First Reich and Second Reich were previous empires when Germany was considered powerful, so Hitler wanted to emphasize that under his rule, Germany would become great and powerful again.

The "Final Solution"

The era of the Third Reich only lasted 12 years, from 1933 to 1945. However, that was long enough to leave a trail of death and destruction in its wake. During this period, Hitler and the Nazi Party attempted to exterminate the Jews of Europe through systematic, state-sponsored mass murder. This has become known to the world as the Holocaust, but the Nazis called it the "Final Solution to the Jewish Question." Today, we know it also as one of the most brutal examples of genocide—the mass killing of members of a particular group or groups of people. In fact, the word "genocide" was first used in 1944 to talk about the Holocaust.

Although the Jewish population was the most brutally and infamously targeted group, they were not the only ones who suffered under the Nazis. The Third Reich was a totalitarian regime—asserting total control over all aspects of society—that targeted many other so-called enemies of the Reich for persecution or extermination. This included the Romani people (also called the Roma), LGBTQ+ people, Jehovah's Witnesses, the mentally and physically disabled, Communists, and political critics.

The most notorious symbol of Nazi brutality was its network of concentration camps within Germany, such as Dachau, Bergen-Belsen, and Buchenwald, and the six extermination camps in Nazi-occupied Poland—Belzec, Chelmno, Majdanek, Sobibor, Treblinka, and the largest of all, Auschwitz. Concentration camps were generally known as places where prisoners were forced to live and work in subhuman conditions. Some would become known as extermination camps (also known as killing centers or death camps) because they were places where people, especially Jewish people, were taken specifically to be murdered.

The Atrocities of Auschwitz

International Holocaust Remembrance Day is January 27 because that is the day Auschwitz was liberated from Nazi control. It was the largest extermination camp and remains the most infamous, standing as a symbol of the atrocities of the Holocaust. Auschwitz was located 37 miles (60 kilometers) west of Kraków, in Nazi-occupied Poland. Formerly an army barracks site, the camp was opened in 1940 as a prison for German criminals and Polish prisoners of war. By the time Allied forces liberated it in 1945, it had become a sprawling complex of around 44 subcamps divided between three main camps. Of these main camps, Auschwitz-Birkenau was the largest and perhaps most infamous as a killing center.

Historians believe between 1.1 million and 1.6 million people died within the walls of the Auschwitz complex. Of these victims, 960,000, or 90 percent, were Jewish. Others murdered include 74,000 non-Jewish Poles, 21,000 Romani, 15,000 Soviets,

These railroad tracks carried millions of people to their deaths at Auschwitz.

and 10,000 to 15,000 Czechs, French, Germans, Austrians, and Yugoslavs.

While hundreds of thousands of people died from starvation, disease, and individual acts of violence at Auschwitz, most died in execution chambers designed specifically for mass murder. To carry out their Final Solution, the Nazis herded prisoners into what looked like shower rooms, sealed the windows and doors, and released Zyklon B—which created a deadly gas—into the chamber, killing those inside quickly. This assembly line of death continued as the dead bodies were moved into crematoria, where large ovens turned them into ash.

Learning from the Past

Although mass murder was carried out at many other camps throughout the lands Germany occupied during World War II, the crimes against humanity that took place at Auschwitz have remained the most well known. However, as of 2018, 66 percent of U.S. adults between the ages of 25 and 40 were not sure what Auschwitz was.

Learning about what happened within the walls of Auschwitz is an essential part of understanding the Holocaust and those who suffered under the Nazi regime. The ideas that led to the Final Solution and camps such as Auschwitz had deep roots in European history but were brought to the surface by Hitler and the Nazis. Anti-Semitism existed long before Hitler and the Holocaust, but the Nazis encouraged mass hysteria about the imagined dangers presented by people of Jewish heritage. This led to discrimination against the Jewish people, violence, and ultimately, genocide at Auschwitz and other camps.

Auschwitz stands as a reminder of the dangers of totalitarianism and the power of propaganda, and it represents perhaps the greatest atrocity in recorded history. In addition, it stands as an acknowledgment of the suffering of the survivors, but also of their will to live, their adaptability in the face of destruction, and a sense of responsibility to make sure the tragedy is neither forgotten nor repeated.

Despite the thousands of memorials built to commemorate the murder of so many people at Auschwitz and other death camps during the Holocaust and the powerful testimonies of the survivors, the forces that produced the Holocaust are still at work around the world today. Experts believe many of them—including anti-Semitism—are growing stronger. That is why it is more important now than ever before to take a deep look into the history of the Holocaust and the camps, especially Auschwitz, where its horrors were carried out.

TELEFUNK

CHAPTER ONE

THE ROAD TO WAR

One of the most common questions asked when learning about the Holocaust is both simple and complex: How could this happen? It is hard to imagine people in Germany turning a blind eye to what was taking place in their own country, and it is hard to believe other countries did not immediately try to stop what was occurring under Hitler's regime. The Holocaust seems like it should have been the driving force behind World War II, with countries around the world stepping in to stop the Nazis' plan of genocide. However, the invasion of Poland by the Nazis in 1939 was actually the reason most nations got involved in the fight. The United States did not enter the war until two years later, after Japan bombed the Pearl Harbor naval base in Hawaii.

Secrecy played a big part in the lack of national and international reaction to the Holocaust until the plan for the Final Solution was well underway. Allied countries did not find out about the widespread murders until 1942. Germans knew that Jewish people were being targeted and discriminated against, and many supported this treatment because of the Nazis' highly effective anti-Jewish propaganda campaign. However, the Nazis kept the exact plan for the

Many German citizens supported Adolf Hitler because they believed he would make their lives better. When he blamed the Jewish people for Germany's problems, these citizens believed him, which allowed the Nazi Party to carry out the Final Solution without much resistance.

Final Solution a secret from their own people for many years, and most average German citizens did not know or believe that their government was systematically murdering people. As the United States Holocaust Memorial Museum (USHMM) reports:

> *Despite the public broadcast and publication of general statements about the goal of eliminating 'the Jews,' the regime practiced a propaganda of deception by hiding specific details about the 'Final Solution' ... At the same time, positive stories were fabricated as part of the planned deception. One booklet printed in 1941 glowingly reported that, in occupied Poland, German authorities had put Jews to work, built clean hospitals, set up soup kitchens for Jews, and provided them with newspapers and vocational training.*[1]

People who lived near the concentration camps almost certainly knew about them, but most chose to remain silent. This was due to a variety of reasons, including fear for their own families and support for Hitler's policies.

Both the design and implementation of the Holocaust—also known by the word Shoah, from a Hebrew word for "catastrophe"—involved conscious and subconscious choices to ignore the humanity of others. Nazi commanders, low-level guards, and ordinary citizens all played a part in the systematic murder of millions of people—some through direct action and others by willfully disregarding what was happening in their own country. They were motivated by German nationalism and deep-seated prejudice against the Jewish people. These were not new forces; they had existed for hundreds of years.

Prejudice and Persecution

Jewish people have faced violence, prejudice, and forced removal from their homes for centuries. Although the Old Testament of the Bible claims the Jews as God's chosen people, it also describes periods of slavery, conquest, and hardship. The persecution of Jews in Europe corresponds with the rise of Christianity in the Roman Empire and Christian portrayals of Jews as the murderers of Jesus

Christ. As the Christian church established itself as the most powerful institution in Europe, Jews and other minority groups were targeted as the enemies of Christianity. During the Crusades, which extended through the 11th, 12th, and 13th centuries, Jews were killed in large numbers in present-day Germany. A century later, Jews were blamed for plague outbreaks that devastated Europe and were consequently banished from many communities and sometimes murdered. By the 1400s, persecution by the Inquisition of the Catholic Church left Jews impoverished and vulnerable to organized massacres called pogroms. Such treatment continued in Russia in the 1800s and early 1900s.

Despite this treatment and their limited opportunities, Jews remained vital to European communities as laborers, politicians, businesspeople, and taxpayers. By the mid-19th century, their numbers were growing again, especially in Europe.

Germany's fortunes were rising, too, at this time. In 1871, through a combination of diplomacy and warfare, chief minister Otto von Bismarck unified the separate states within German territory into one. The nation led the world as an industrial power, its strength virtually unrivaled in Europe. However, powerful political rivalries would soon plunge all of Europe into war, and European Jews would be on the defensive once again.

Looking for Someone to Blame

World War I, a global conflict pitting the Central Powers (led by Germany, Austria-Hungary, and the Ottoman Empire of the Turks) against the Allies (led by the British Empire, Russia, France, Italy, and the United States), devastated the continent for four years, beginning in 1914. The conflict killed more than 20 million soldiers and civilians, injured 20 million more, and tore apart an entire generation. Although anti-Semitism began generations before, World War I brought discrimination and the casting of blame into sharper focus.

Jews in Austria and Germany had initially been caught up in the war effort as proud citizens. Thousands volunteered and fought in World War I, and approximately 12,000 of them died in the service of their country. However, as Germany began losing the war, Jews were accused of undermining the country, avoiding military service, and being inferior soldiers. The nation was looking for culprits for the humiliating loss, and Jews, despite their proven patriotism, became an easy target. This was yet another example in the long history of Jews becoming scapegoats for problems in Europe, and it foreshadowed how scapegoating would play a large role in the development of the Final Solution.

The Treaty of Versailles, signed on June 28, 1919, officially ended the war between Germany and the Allies. Its key clauses placed the entire blame for the war on Germany, ordered the dismantling of Germany's armed forces and the ceding of territory to Allied nations, and required Germany to pay billions of dollars in war reparations to the victorious Allies. The German politicians who oversaw the surrender of Germany in November 1918 and the signing of Treaty of Versailles—labeled "November criminals" in the German press—were, like the Jews, considered traitors by a nation looking for people to blame for their losses.

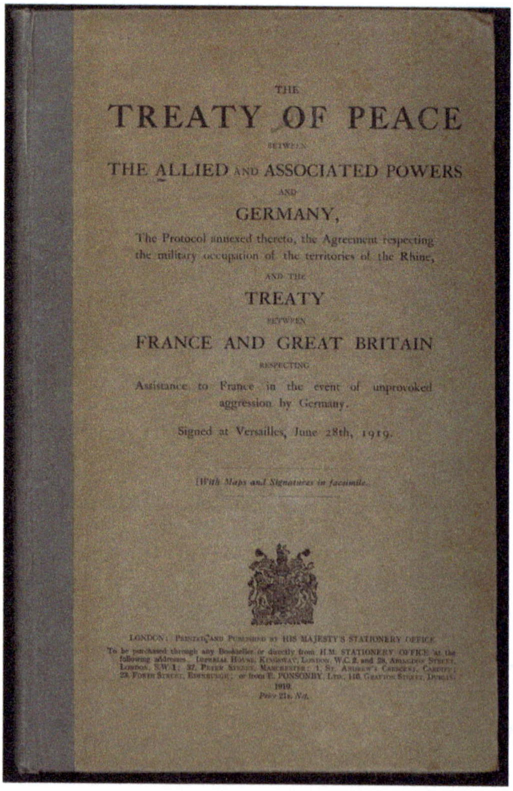
THE
TREATY OF PEACE
BETWEEN
THE ALLIED AND ASSOCIATED POWERS
AND
GERMANY,
The Protocol annexed thereto, the Agreement respecting the military occupation of the territories of the Rhine,
AND THE
TREATY
BETWEEN
FRANCE AND GREAT BRITAIN
RESPECTING
Assistance to France in the event of unprovoked aggression by Germany.
Signed at Versailles, June 28th, 1919.
[With Maps and Signatures in facsimile.]
LONDON: PRINTED AND PUBLISHED BY HIS MAJESTY'S STATIONERY OFFICE.
1919.

Shown here is a copy of the Treaty of Versailles, which ended World War I but laid the groundwork for problems that would lead to World War II.

Nazi Nationalism

After World War I, Germany was a nation in ruins. The new postwar government was called the Weimar Republic. It remained mostly

FROM THE SOURCE: THE TREATY OF VERSAILLES

The Treaty of Versailles, signed at the end of World War I, reduced the territory of Germany and outlined many conditions and declarations the country was forced to accept, including Article 231, the so-called War Guilt Clause:

> *The Allied and Associated Governments affirm and Germany accepts the responsibility of Germany and her allies for causing all the loss and damage to which the Allied and Associated Governments and their nationals have been subjected as a consequence of the war imposed upon them by the aggression of Germany and her allies.*

Other sections of the treaty focused on how Germany would make reparations to the Allied nations, amounting to billions of dollars:

> *The Allied and Associated Governments, however, require, and Germany undertakes, that she will make compensation for all damage done to the civilian population of the Allied and Associated Powers and to their property during the period of the belligerency of each as an Allied or Associated Power against Germany by such aggression by land, by sea and from the air, and in general all damage as defined.*[1]

1. "Treaty of Peace with Germany (Treaty of Versailles)," Library of Congress, pp. 137–138, www.loc.gov/law/help/us-treaties/bevans/m-ust000002-0043.pdf (accessed January 5, 2021).

ineffective between 1919 and 1932. Jobs were few, poverty rose, and a national feeling of despair and humiliation descended on the once-proud country.

The stage was set for the rise of an ideology—and a leader—that promised to restore Germany's wealth and greatness. The leader was Austrian-born Adolf Hitler, a failed art student, anti-Semite, and decorated Bavarian corporal during World War I. After the war, Hitler found his political voice in Munich, Germany, as part of the German Workers' Party, which would later become the Nazi Party.

In 1920, Hitler and his closest aides developed a 25-point program by which the Nazi Party would operate, including the abandonment of the terms of the Treaty of Versailles and the expansion of Germany into new lands. Hitler envisioned not simply a form of government, but an empire that would last for a thousand years. His empire would be built on discrimination against the Jews, as the 25-point plan featured strong anti-Semitic language. The essence of Nazi ideology was, therefore, based on a combination of racism and nationalism.

In 1923, after more than three years of openly railing against the failures of the Weimar Republic, Hitler and 600 of his supporters turned their ideas into bold action. Armed with machine guns, they stormed a tavern in Munich in an attempt to take control of the republic. The coup quickly devolved into confusion and gunfire. The Beer Hall Putsch, as it came to be known, resulted in the deaths of 16 Nazi Party supporters and 4 Bavarian police officers. The trial that followed and Hitler's fiery testimony on the stand made him a

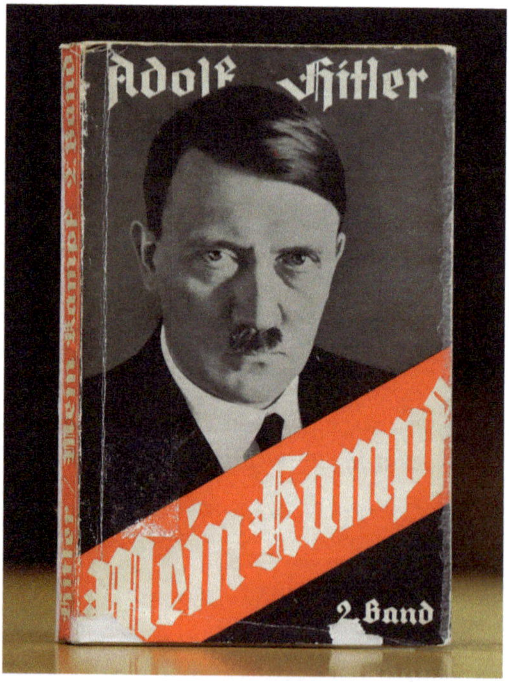

By the end of 1939, Adolf Hitler's only book, *Mein Kampf*, had sold more than 5 million copies. While not considered a well-written work, it explained Hitler's ideas for Germany's rebirth.

national celebrity and a favorite of the presiding judge. Despite a five-year prison sentence, Hitler was released after less than a year. The young leader used his time in jail to put his political ideas to paper. Published in two volumes in 1925 and 1927, Hitler's book *Mein Kampf* (*My Struggle*) sold poorly. However, as Hitler's popularity grew, the book came to be seen as his master plan for Germany and for the annihilation of the Jewish people.

Although Hitler's Nazi Party promised the people of Germany economic stability and a renewed sense of purpose, his fiery speeches before ever-growing crowds also stoked the flames of German nationalism and dripped with contempt for Communists and Jews. However, because the Nazi Party did not lead with its anti-Semitic agenda and instead focused on Germany's return to power and protection for German workers, Germans were inclined to support the party. It continued to grow in popularity.

Hitler's Promises

Hitler's rise to the chancellorship of the Weimar Republic in January 1933 was viewed by many Germans as a national rebirth. Germans now had something—and someone—to believe in. Hitler promised to protect and defend the German people from invasion; he promised to rebuild the nation's economy and put citizens to work. He also promised to destroy all enemies of the state.

Now, with a mandate from the German people, he was intent on carrying those principles out. Upon his swearing in as chancellor, Hitler quickly consolidated power in line with his aim of putting all aspects of German society—politics, culture, education, the economy, the press, and more—under the control of the Nazi Party and stamping out all resistance.

In March 1933, two months after Hitler assumed the chancellorship of Germany, the first Nazi concentration camp opened in Dachau, near Munich. Its early prisoners were mostly political opponents of the new regime, but as the march to the nation's renewal began, Germany's Jewish citizens had much to fear.

Nazi Propaganda

This is an example of the stars that Jews were forced to wear in Germany under the Third Reich to easily identify them.

With his party now in control of the country's newspapers and radio outlets, Hitler's message of reunifying the German nation, torn apart by World War I, struck a chord with many Germans. Otto Dietrich, the Third Reich press chief, led the charge "to enrage Germans against the Jews," according to the court transcripts of a post–World War II trial, "to justify the measures taken and to be taken against them, and to subdue any doubts which might arise as to the justice of measures of racial persecution to which Jews were to be subjected."[2]

Founded on the premise that Germanic blood and Jewish blood were fundamentally different, the Nazi Party devised a plan to alienate an entire people. This plan—called Aryanization—was designed to repress Jews both socially and economically. On April 1, 1933, the Nazis began a boycott of Jewish-owned businesses. Carrying signs reading "The Jews Are Our Misfortune" and "Don't Buy from Jews," Hitler's brown-shirted paramilitary group, an armed force known as the SA (*Sturmabteilung* in German, "storm troopers" in English), scrawled the word *Jude* (German for "Jew") as well as yellow and black Stars of David across shop doors and windows. Jewish people were beaten and taunted. A week later, the new government put race laws in place that segregated and discriminated against Jewish citizens. Many literally saw the writing on the wall. In 1933, more than 37,000 Jews emigrated from Germany. Others—either too poor to relocate or hopeful that things would improve—stayed. Germany was their home, after all.

PAST MEETS PRESENT: JUDAISM—RACE OR RELIGION?

Hitler based his justification for the Final Solution on the idea that the Jews were genetically inferior to what he called the Aryan race, by which he meant a pure German race. By calling the Jews a race, Hitler made them separate from the rest of the Germans and created a group that could take the blame for anything he wanted. He defined a Jewish person as anyone with three or four Jewish grandparents, completely ignoring religious beliefs. A person who was raised as a Christian and went to church regularly but had three Jewish grandparents could still be sent to a concentration camp.

Even today, there is debate about whether Judaism is a race or a religion. Most Jews will agree that although they share a common history and culture, they are not a race because anyone can convert to Judaism. However, the issue is complicated by the fact that a person born to a Jewish mother is considered Jewish by more traditional or religiously observant individuals, even if that person does not practice Judaism. However, other people may only consider them to be Jewish if they practice the Jewish religion.

Also significant to the discussion is the agreement among most scientists that race is a social construct. It has no biological basis, and in fact, there is very little genetic diversity among humans. Therefore, Hitler's contention that Jews were genetically inferior had no foundation in reality.

The Notorious Nuremberg Laws

By 1934, the situation had worsened. Now, after purging his enemies within the government, Hitler became führer, commander of both the political and military wings of the Third Reich. With his new dictatorial powers, and 90 percent of the 45.5 million voting Germans behind him, he escalated his policies against the Jews.

In 1935, the party enacted the Nuremberg Laws. The acts claimed Jews were a separate race defined by birth and by blood and stripped them of German citizenship. The idea of racial purity soon became a symbol of prejudice against Jews. Stripped of the benefits of citizenship, Jews were subjected to blatant acts of anti-Semitism. Marriage between Jews and non-Jews was forbidden, Jewish university professors were fired from their jobs, supporting Jewish-owned businesses was banned, and Jews could no longer employ German maids under the age of 45. (A racist fear among some Germans that Jewish men might corrupt young German females was promoted in Nazi propaganda, which spread lies about what Jewish people were like.)

Other racist Jewish stereotypes such as long, crooked noses, wide mouths, and a lust for money took hold in the minds of many Germans during this time, supported by images in Nazi propaganda. These notions, combined with the legal definition of what a Jew was, became an obsession in the new Germany. Doctors measured a person's features with sharp metal instruments, and one's ancestry became of utmost importance. People flooded church registries and sought out birth certificates to determine how much, if any, Jewish blood ran through their veins.

Such hysteria even found its way into children's books. One example from a 1936 publication read in part:

The Devil is the father of the Jew.
When God created the world,
He invented the races:
The Indians, the Negroes [Black people], the Chinese
And also the wicked creature called the Jew.[3]

Kristallnacht

A turning point in the Nazis' war against the Jews occurred in Paris, France, on November 3, 1938. That day, 17-year-old Polish Jew Herschel Grynszpan received a desperate letter from his sister, Berta, in Germany, saying that the Grynszpan family was being deported back to Poland under direct orders from the Nazi regime. Quick-tempered and impulsive, Herschel Grynszpan fretted about what to do. His family had struggled to survive in the German city of Hanover for 28 years. Now, they were being thrown out.

Three days after receiving the letter, Grynszpan left his apartment. He checked into the Hotel de Suez and stayed the night. After breakfast on the morning of November 7, he made his way to a gun shop in the Saint Martin district of Paris and purchased a pistol. Grynszpan took a train to the German embassy and asked to see an embassy official. He had an important document for him, he said. After being shown into Secretary Ernst vom Rath's office, Grynszpan pulled his gun from his pocket and fired five times at vom Rath. Vom Rath died two days later. When asked about his act of revenge against Germany for its treatment of the Jews, Grynszpan said, "It is not, after all, a crime to be Jewish. I am not a dog. I have the right to live. My people have a right to exist on this earth."[4]

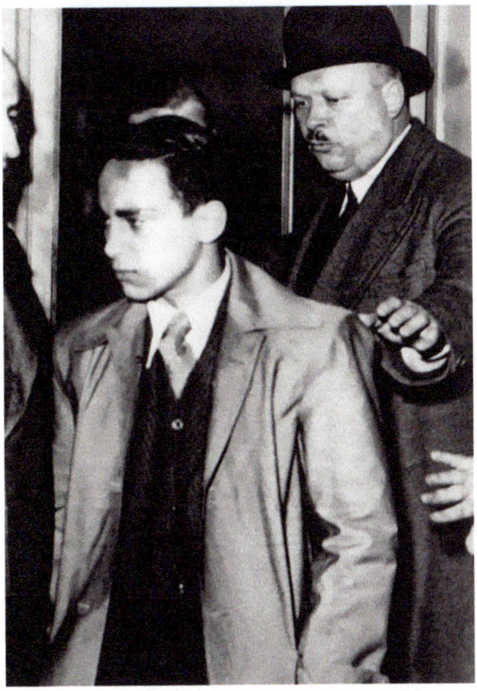

Herschel Grynszpan is shown with French police after being arrested for the assassination of Ernst vom Rath. Following Germany's invasion of France, the Nazis took Grynszpan into custody. Some think the Nazis killed him at some point, but no one knows for sure.

News of the assassination spread quickly. The German, Nazi-controlled press made sure its readers knew that a Jew was responsible. The murder became an excuse to unleash more hatred and violence on the entire Jewish population.

Throughout the night of November 9 to 10, 1938, the skies across Germany and Austria were set ablaze by soldiers and people on the streets. In the event known as Kristallnacht, or "Night of Broken Glass," about 7,500 Jewish-owned businesses had their windows smashed, hundreds of synagogues were burned, cemeteries were desecrated, and Jewish citizens were dragged from their houses and beaten. More than 90 Jewish people died. In most places, firefighters watched, told to only stop the fires from spreading to non-Jewish areas.

An example of how tightly the Nazis controlled aspects of German culture, the 1940 film *Jud Süss* (translated "Süss the Jew"), considered one of the most anti-Semitic movies of all time, was enormously popular in Germany.

On January 25, 1939, German foreign minister Joachim von Ribbentrop distributed a circular that contained what was perhaps the most direct evidence yet of what the Nazis had in store for Europe's Jewish populace: "It is not by chance that 1938, the year of our destiny, saw the realization of our plan for Greater Germany as well as a major step towards the solution of the Jewish problem."[5]

An Eye on Expansion

The Third Reich wanted to go to war to increase the size of Germany. This militarism and territorial expansion was justified under the banner of Lebensraum, or "living space," which Hitler portrayed as Germany's destiny. Hitler's regime also claimed the right to reclaim territory that had been taken from Germany under the terms of the Treaty of Versailles.

On March 12, 1938, Germany took an important, aggressive step by sending troops across the border into Austria, incorporating

THEY MADE HISTORY: JOSEPH GOEBBELS, THE MAN BEHIND NAZI PROPAGANDA

Propaganda was so important to the German Third Reich that a government position was created to oversee it: minister of propaganda. The infamous holder of this position was Joseph Goebbels. Born in 1897, Goebbels was a German nationalist, but he seemingly was not anti-Semitic at first. In fact, he valued his Jewish teachers and was once engaged to a Jewish woman.

However, when he became involved in politics, eventually backing Adolf Hitler's ambitions, his efforts turned to gathering support for Hitler's platform and turning public opinion against Jews. Goebbels became head of the National Ministry for Public Enlightenment and Propaganda. He oversaw German press, radio, theater, films, literature, music, and fine arts, all of which he used as tools for propaganda when possible.

As World War II waged on, Goebbels was charged with maintaining the Germans' belief that they could still be victorious even after suffering great losses. To do this, he falsely suggested the Nazis had secret weapons they had not yet used and took other measures as well. After Hitler's suicide, Goebbels became chancellor of Germany—for one day. On May 1, 1945, he and his wife had their children poisoned to death and then killed themselves.

the neighboring country in an operation known as Anschluss, or "union." Hitler desired to do the same with much of eastern Europe. As he strengthened his army in violation of the treaty, Joachim von Ribbentrop and Soviet foreign minister Vyacheslav Mikhaylovich Molotov signed the German-Soviet Nonaggression Pact in August 1939 in the presence of Soviet dictator Joseph Stalin. This planned 10-year agreement stated that the two countries would not attack one another. It also contained a secret protocol that divided Poland

Hitler is shown here being greeted enthusiastically by large crowds in Vienna, Austria, days after annexing the country.

and the rest of eastern Europe into German and Soviet spheres of influence. The pact became the first step toward a proposed domination of all of Europe by the two powers.

Other European nations, including Great Britain, at first refused to believe the rumors of an agreement between the two bitter enemies. British Prime Minister Neville Chamberlain told his cabinet only a month before that he did not think such an alliance was possible. Hitler wasted little time in proving Chamberlain wrong.

The Invasion of Poland

On September 1, 1939, Germany invaded Poland and claimed it as part of "Greater Germany." The bombing by the German air force (Luftwaffe) of the city of Wieluń began the "September Campaign," as many Poles called it. German ground and sea forces attacked Polish towns and military installations too. In an attempt to justify their military actions, Nazi propagandists asserted—falsely—that

Poland had been planning, along with Great Britain and France, to dismantle Germany. They also claimed that Poles were oppressing Germans. Thus, Hitler attempted to make his campaign of aggression look like retaliation.

A young Jewish Pole named William Luksenburg watched the events during the first night of the invasion. He witnessed one of his neighbors crossing a street in his town, disobeying German orders. A German soldier yelled for the young man to stop, but the neighbor began running. The soldier shot and killed the youth with a machine gun in front of the Luksenburg house. Soldiers ordered Luksenburg and four others to take the body away. When he got home afterward, he found himself soaked in the young man's blood. He recalled, "I [will] always remember my mother's . . . expression and my mother's fear and my mother's cry out when she saw me completely covered with blood and that was the first night . . . We didn't know what [was] coming."[6]

The German army entered Warsaw, Poland, in 1939. The damage from German airstrikes is visible in buildings in the background of this photo.

HISTORY HAPPENED HERE: WIELUŃ, POLAND

The attack on Wieluń, Poland, was the first major action of World War II. Wieluń was 12 miles (19.3 km) from the German border. While Germany was gearing up for war in the years before the strike, no one thought the Polish town was in danger. It did not seem to serve a strategic purpose for the Germans and was defended by few Polish soldiers. However, the attacks by the German Luftwaffe served to demonstrate the power of the German air force, having destroyed more than 70 percent of the town—including a well-marked hospital—and killed hundreds of its inhabitants. Because of the great civilian loss of life, many consider the attack to be Germany's first war crime of the conflict.

Wieluń was later rebuilt, but the bombing is still solemnly remembered by the Polish people. An exhibit dedicated to this early event of World War II is installed at the Bundeswehr Military History Museum in Dresden, Germany.

Great Britain and France were among the first nations to declare war against Germany for its actions. Still, with the aid of the Soviet Union, the Nazis overran Poland in about a month. This new war seemed an echo of the first world war at the start. However, in this one, Hitler was seeking to wipe out the Third Reich's enemies, Jewish people among them.

Months before, in January 1939, Hitler linked the looming war not to his own exploits but to the Jews. In a speech at the Reichstag, he asserted, "If international finance and Jewry inside and outside Europe should succeed in plunging the nations once more into a world war, the result will be not … the victory of Jewry, but the annihilation of the Jewish race in Europe."[7]

Though the German Jewish population had dwindled by 1939, the invasion of Poland gave the Nazis control of a Polish Jewish population of more than 3 million. The persecution that had forced

German Jews to flee their country was now applied to Polish Jews. They had to identify themselves by wearing armbands with the Star of David. Their businesses and properties were taken away. They were forced into areas called ghettos to separate them from the general population. Even more devastating plans would soon be set in motion for the Polish Jews as the Nazis—even as they sought to expand into farther regions of the continent—maintained their objective of a Europe free of Jewish people.

How You See History

1. What conditions in Germany made Hitler's rise to power possible?
2. Do you think Kristallnacht would have occurred if Herschel Grynszpan had not assassinated Ernst vom Rath? Why or why not?
3. How did German citizens participate in the persecution of Jews before World War II?

CHAPTER TWO

VIOLENCE AND TERROR

The violence against the Jews in Germany and German-held territory was not immediately apparent to outsiders. Hitler did not campaign on the promise of killing Jewish people. If he had done this, his message might have informed other countries of his plans. Instead, he let ordinary people take out their frustrations on Jewish members of their communities and slowly disseminated, through propaganda and laws, the idea that Jews were not worthy of respect and dignity. Thus, Hitler's campaign was insidious.

The Nuremberg Laws had made German Jews subjects of the state but not citizens, stripping them of any civil rights. The Jews suffered humiliations both small and large. Sometimes their aggressors were neighbors they had known their whole lives, who now identified them as enemies.

This cruelty would later translate into Jews being rounded up and forced into run-down sections of cities called ghettos. Yet still, even isolated and powerless like this, the Third Reich viewed them as a problem to be solved. They would be taken from the ghettos and transported to camps, where the Final Solution would be revealed to be their mass murder.

Heinrich Himmler was sometimes called the second-most powerful man in the Third Reich, after Hitler. He played a large part in the Final Solution.

Separating Jews from Society

Heinrich Himmler, Hitler's second in command, was an innocent-looking but ruthless Nazi commander obsessed with racial purity. He longed to weed out non-Aryans from the ranks of the German people he claimed to serve. As he built his police forces in the years leading up to World War II, his perfect specimens had to meet certain requirements. They had to be at least 5 feet 8 inches (173 centimeters) in height and be able to trace their racially pure Germanic ancestry back to at least 1800—or to 1750 for officers.

Himmler was always looking for more effective and more impersonal methods of ridding Germany of Jews. Initially, deportation, perhaps to Africa, seemed like a good plan. However, transporting millions of people to another continent quickly proved impractical for the Nazis. At first, the government encouraged the Jews to emigrate, or leave on their own, but many could not because other countries were unwilling to let them in. The Nazis also saw the Jews' property as being rightfully owned by the Third Reich, so although they made it easy for Jews to leave the country, they made it very difficult for them to take any of their money or belongings. This meant that many Jews could not afford to leave even if they could find somewhere to go. Emigration was eventually banned in 1941.

An answer to the Nazis' Jewish problem eventually came from another Nazi official, SS lieutenant colonel Adolf Eichmann, who devised the idea of confining Jews to massive European ghettos. Eichmann, Himmler, and Hitler soon came to believe that Jews could at least be kept separate from the rest of the population.

Less than four months after Germany's invasion of Poland, the first large-scale Jewish ghetto was established in the Polish city of Tuliszków. Ghettos in Lodz and Warsaw soon followed. The ghettos—which had ramshackle tenement buildings with no heat and little drinking water—were walled off from the rest of the city in which they were located. Those trying to escape were typically shot. Warsaw held the largest of these cramped and dirty places, eventually housing nearly 30 percent of the population in only 2.4 percent of the city's area.

Life in the ghetto was a daily struggle to survive. Food was scarce and sanitation nearly nonexistent. Garbage was everywhere.

Emmanuel Ringelblum learned the horrors firsthand while living in the Warsaw ghetto. Ringelblum felt the worst part of the experience was seeing children freezing in the wintertime. "They whine, beg, sing, lament and tremble in the cold," he wrote in his diary, "without underwear, without clothes, without shoes, covered only by rags and bags which are tied by strings to meager skeletons."[1]

Nazi leaders viewed the ghettos as the first step on the road toward Jewish eradication. Before long, as overcrowding resulted in starvation and death, they devised more reliable methods of destruction.

A little more than a year after the first Nazi-controlled ghetto was established in Tuliszków, Himmler received a document containing statistics on the number of Jews remaining in the German Reich. Distributed on December 4, 1940, the report suggested transferring "the Jews out of the European economic space of the German people to a still-to-be-determined territory."[2] Such a plan would involve the deportation of millions.

This photograph shows the terrible conditions of the Warsaw ghetto after the war ended, in 1946.

Hiding for Their Lives

According to the Anne Frank Museum, about 28,000 Jews went into hiding in the Netherlands because they were unable to leave the country. This was not an option for most people; it was hard for them to find non-Jews who were willing to risk their own lives by illegally hiding them. It was rare for whole families to go into hiding together. Many adults would try to save their children by placing them with a sympathetic family. Provided the child could pass as an Aryan, they would need false papers, which were extremely difficult to get. When the papers could not be obtained or the child looked Jewish enough to create suspicion, the only option was to live in cellars, attics, or barns. They had to be quiet all the time and could rarely leave their hiding spots.

The most famous story of Jews in hiding is that of Anne Frank, her family, and the four others invited to join them. These eight people lived for two years in a secret annex behind a bookshelf. Otto Frank's four employees helped by bringing them food and other supplies. Unlike most people who were forced into hiding, the Franks and their friends had a two-floor apartment. However, being unable to leave it for so long was difficult for all of them. Eventually, an unknown informant betrayed them, and most of them were sent to Auschwitz. Otto Frank was the only one to survive.

Forces of Terror

Jewish ghettos were only part of the plan for European Jews. Soon after Poland fell, the Nazis sent out their most loyal guard—a paramilitary police force of some 250,000 men known as the Schutzstaffel, or SS—to root out and destroy all enemies of the German state. The SS was originally a small force that served as Hitler's personal bodyguards; now, under the leadership of Heinrich Himmler, SS units became the administrators of the occupied territories and Hitler's network of concentration and labor camps. They had free rein to persecute and brutalize those of Jewish descent, prisoners of war, and any individuals bold enough to disagree with the Third Reich's policies. These death squads murdered more than 15,000 Poles.

HISTORY HAPPENED HERE: THE ANNE FRANK HOUSE

Today, the 17th-century building in which the Frank family hid from Nazi persecution in the Netherlands is a museum open to the public. The building, which had been the home of Otto Frank's businesses, is located in Amsterdam on a canal called the Prinsengracht. It was nearly demolished after the war but was saved by a group of people, including Otto Frank, who believed it should be preserved because of its history.

After the Franks had been arrested and sent to concentration camps, friends found some personal items they had left behind. These included young Anne's diary, which would prove invaluable in helping other people understand life at that time for Jews in German territory. Since 1960, people can visit the building and even go into the secret annex in the back of the house where the Franks lived for 761 days. More than 1 million people visit the Anne Frank House each year.

Additional mobile killing units called Einsatzgruppen were activated to follow the German armies on the eastern front and kill saboteurs, Jews, and Communists. Divided into four battalion-size groups labeled A through D, the Einsatzgruppen conducted a reign of terror that many historians view as the forerunner of, and parallel to, the systematic murder of innocent civilians that would soon be institutionalized in the death camps.

Some Nazi commanders hesitated to kill civilians, not because they felt the murder of innocents was wrong, but because they were not sure their men could carry out such orders and not be physically sickened. Soldiers are trained to gaze down the barrel of their rifles and shoot armed enemies. This would be different—their victims would carry no weapons and pose no physical threat. They were marked for death only because the Nazi state said so.

Einsatzgruppen officers, therefore, often prepared their men through a "stepwise escalation of the killing," said scholar

FROM THE SOURCE: ANNE FRANK'S DIARY

In 1947, the diary of Anne Frank was published as *Het Achterhuis* (*The Secret Annex*). It has since become one of the most widely read books from that time, a glimpse into what life was like for a young Jewish girl in hiding during World War II. The difficulties of such a secret life are clear in an entry in 1942:

> *The fact that we can never go outside bothers me more than I can say, and then I'm really afraid that we'll be discovered and shot, not a very nice prospect, needless to say.*

In her last entry, in August 1944, before her family was discovered and arrested, she wrote:

> *I simply can't build up my hopes on a foundation consisting of confusion, misery and death, I see the world gradually being turned into a wilderness, I hear the ever approaching thunder, which will destroy us too, I can feel the sufferings of millions and yet, if I look up*

Daniel Jonah Goldhagen. "First, by shooting primarily teenage and adult Jewish males, they would be able to acclimate themselves to mass executions without the shock of killing women, young children, and the infirm."[3]

In their roundups, German officers and soldiers took advantage of the anti-Semitism long ingrained in small villages across eastern Europe. With the help of local Ukrainian, Latvian, and Lithuanian informants, the Einsatzgruppen identified the Jews and Romani in an occupied area. Houses were attacked, and victims were dragged into the streets and then marched or driven to execution sites, often simple ravines or fields into which long trenches had already been dug. Sometimes the terrified victims were forced at gunpoint

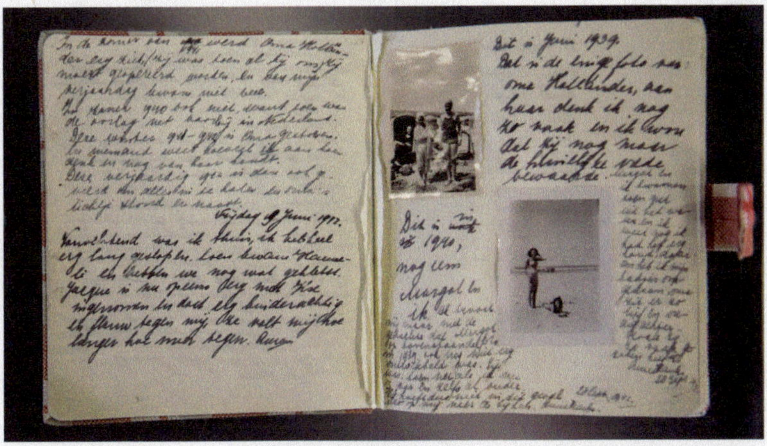

This is a copy of Anne Frank's handwritten diary. She received the diary as a gift on her 13th birthday from her parents in 1942.

into the heavens, I think that it will all come right, that this cruelty too will end, and that peace and tranquility will return again. In the meantime, I must uphold my ideals, for perhaps the time will come when I shall be able to carry them out.[1]

1. Quoted in "Anne Frank: Diary," United States Holocaust Memorial Museum, encyclopedia.ushmm.org/content/en/article/anne-frank-diary (accessed January 11, 2020).

to dig the holes themselves. All were ordered to hand over any rings, bracelets, watches, wallets, and money—anything of value—and remove their clothes. After lining up in front of the trenches, these naked, frightened villagers were mowed down by machine-gun fire. Bulldozers or men with shovels filled in the trenches.

The murderers themselves, many no older than 18 or 20, responded in various ways to their morbid task. Hans Friedrich, a member of an SS infantry unit supporting the Einsatzgruppen in the Ukraine, reported his unit experienced little or no resistance from the victims. Friedrich willingly admitted to shooting Jews, Romani, and others. Although more than a million Jews and tens of thousands of Romani, Communist officials, and disabled people died at

This photograph shows an SS force about to execute Jews from Kiev in 1941. The ditch below them already contains victims.

the hands of the Einsatzgruppen, Friedrich claimed to feel no sense of remorse. Nor, he said, had he lost one night of sleep thinking about it.

The T4 Program

T4, the Nazi involuntary euthanasia program, began in the fall of 1939. As Hitler's army poured into Poland, medical staff at six centers checked medical records and decided who would live. Doctors, nurses, and midwives were under orders to register children up to three years of age who appeared mentally disabled, physically deformed, or unusual in any other way. A questionnaire, distributed to those who treated the patients, had to be filled out. Then, medical staff, many of whom had not examined the children themselves, made a decision for or against what Hitler called a "mercy death." A red plus sign indicated a serious defect in the child and a recommendation to kill him or her; a blue minus sign meant the child was to live. Three plus signs meant certain death.

Before long, the program was expanded to include older children and adults, such as those suffering from such mental disorders as

PAST MEETS PRESENT: EUTHANASIA

The word "euthanasia" comes from Greek, in which *eu* means "good" and *thanatos* means "death." It means allowing someone to die more quickly in order to prevent them from suffering further. Usually the person is terminally ill with no available treatments to help them. The three kinds of euthanasia include voluntary, in which a patient requests it; nonvoluntary, in which a patient is not able to give consent but another responsible party gives it for them; and involuntary euthanasia, in which a patient could make a decision about dying but is not asked. The third is considered murder.

The origin of the Nazi euthanasia program was the killing of children with incurable illnesses. They were seen to be a "drain" on state funds. However, later, in the overwhelming majority of cases, the Nazi euthanasia program targeted thousands of people the Nazis deemed to be "unfit" for their society rather than a means to alleviate suffering. These included people with disabilities, mental illnesses, and other nondeadly conditions. Certainly, very few would have chosen death as Nazi doctors chose for them. Officially, this program ended in 1941, after a Catholic bishop in Germany, among others, spoke out against it. However, killing in concentration camps would persist.

Euthanasia remains a controversial issue. It continues to be illegal in most countries. In the United States, only a few states allow doctor-assisted suicide and only in certain cases. Involuntary euthanasia remains strictly banned in nearly all countries.

schizophrenia. The German psychiatric clinic Hadamar became infamous, in large part because of the merciless tactics of its director, Christian Wirth, known to inmates and SS alike by the ironic nickname the "savage Christian."

The euthanasia program became a testing ground for tactics used by the Nazis in the concentration camps later in the war. Perhaps 200,000 people had died by the time the program ceased.

The Opening of Auschwitz

As the mass slaughter in the east continued, the Third Reich also increased the number of concentration camps, which soon dotted the occupied territories of Greater Germany. Many within Germany had already been in operation for eight years. However, with Third Reich forces pushing deeper into new territory, more room for political enemies was needed. The Nazi leadership decided to create a new forced labor camp near a small town in the Upper Silesia region of southwestern Poland.

Considered unsuitable as living space for German citizens because of its barrenness and damp climate, the area near the village of Oświęcim seemed the perfect place for a holding camp—a place in which prisoners would be temporarily kept until being moved to other camps. However, soon after discovering the spot, Nazi officials made the camp permanent. They also translated the Polish Oświęcim into the German Auschwitz.

On May 1, 1940, 39-year-old SS captain Rudolf Höss was made the camp's first commandant. Originally conceived of as a concentration camp, Auschwitz borrowed the procedures and dehumanizing tactics that had been effective at Dachau, Höss's previous post. Theodor Eicke, Dachau's first commandant, specialized in ordered brutality—including beatings and torture. While the average stay for prisoners lasted about a year, Eicke and other officials could shorten or lengthen the sentence at will. Despite the torturous uncertainty, thousands did eventually leave.

Another feature introduced by Eicke at Dachau was Kapos. The word was probably taken from the Italian word *capo*, or "head." Camp officers chose prisoners to lead the separate blocks, or areas of the camp. In an effort to impress their jailers, Kapos could often be crueler than the Nazis themselves. Should they fail to do their jobs, they would quickly be sent back to live with the other inmates—a fate that would mean certain death.

In Dachau, the Nazis first tried to process and manage large groups of people. They also put into practice strict rules, demanding loyalty, unquestioning obedience, and hardness from the guards. Eicke demanded such things, and more: "Anyone who shows even the slightest vestige of sympathy towards them [prisoners] must immediately vanish from our ranks. I need only hard, totally committed SS men. There is no place amongst us for soft people."[4]

Auschwitz's first inmates were 30 German criminals transferred from Sachsenhausen concentration camp in northern Germany. They were quickly made Kapos to help control those who came after them. The Kapos were encouraged by German soldiers to punish the other prisoners harshly. In return for their cruelty, the Kapos were rewarded with cigarettes or soup. Under such circumstances, the new Polish prisoners quickly learned that certain Kapos were better to work for than others.

In short order, Rudolf Höss was ordered to increase the camp's capacity for inmates. His superior, SS commander Oswald Pohl, also suggested Höss integrate the camp into the Reich-owned German Earth and Stone Works as a way of financially supporting itself and Greater Germany. Höss had learned from his own time in prison

Auschwitz's infamous gate, and the sign over it, is still standing for visitors to see.

that work can keep a prisoner alive and help them face the new day while behind bars. Not long after taking command, Höss ordered prisoners to post a message that would become an ironic symbol of the brutality and disguised purpose of Auschwitz. In letters bent out of wrought iron above the camp gate, the sign read: "*Arbeit macht frei*" ("Work makes one free").

Finalizing Their Solution

On January 20, 1942, 15 German government officials and high-ranking Nazis met at a lavish guesthouse in a suburb of Berlin called Wannsee. This secret gathering, now known as the Wannsee Conference, was led by Reinhard Heydrich, chief of the Main Office for the Security of the Reich. After the Nazi officials took time to chat and enjoy refreshments, Heydrich rose to speak. According to minutes taken at the meeting, Heydrich first announced to all in attendance that he had been appointed to lead preparations for the Final Solution.

Heydrich announced that Hitler had authorized the evacuation of the Jews of Europe to the east. He explained how individuals would be divided by sex as well as by their ability to work, building roads. He also noted that a high percentage of Jews would undoubtedly die through this forced labor. One of Heydrich's chief concerns was that large numbers of them might survive the Third Reich's attempt to work them to death. According to historian Laurence Rees, "these were the very Jews that natural selection would have determined were the most dangerous to the Nazis. These Jews, said Heydrich, must also be 'treated accordingly.'"[5] Heydrich and his absent superiors were proposing extermination for Europe's Jewish population.

Gas Chambers

Himmler had already ordered soldiers to begin killing women and children during Einsatzgruppen raids in the east. Himmler added 40,000 more soldiers to the death squads for the purpose of speeding up the process. Another method also looked promising. The technical department of the Reich Security Main Office had developed a process by which up to 40 prisoners could be placed in a sealed van. A metal pipe connected to the exhaust gas hose then pumped carbon monoxide back into the van, killing the people inside in a matter of minutes. Within months, 30 such gas vans, nicknamed "hell vans," traveled across the Baltic countries, Serbia, and Belorussia.

The Einsatzgruppen's operations expanded greatly beginning in June 1941, when Germany invaded its former ally, the Soviet Union, at that time home to possibly 3 million Jews. Betrayed by Hitler, Stalin declared war on Germany and joined the Allies by fighting German armies on a huge new eastern front.

In planning the invasion of Russia, known as Operation Barbarossa, Heydrich ordered all Jews killed regardless of age or gender. However, with additional millions of Jews as well as thousands of Soviet prisoners of war to do away with, small-scale extermination methods such as gassing vans and mass shootings would no longer suffice. Gas chambers made to look like showers were built in a small number of concentration camps that would become known as death camps—because their primary purpose was the systemized extermination of people sent there. The first gas chambers were tested at Chelmno, which opened in December 1941. Other killing centers followed, including Treblinka, Belzec, and Sobibor.

The Nazis and their followers also thought the murder of disabled people made perfect sense. The involuntary euthanasia program, T4, came to Auschwitz on July 28, 1941. A medical commission chose 575 seriously ill, disabled, and elderly prisoners from the hospital. They were taken to a waiting train, transported to a mental hospital in eastern Germany, and gassed. This was the first time that the Nazis used poison to kill Auschwitz prisoners they deemed unfit to work. It would not be the last.

Poisonous Chemical Cocktail

In time, this method of destruction also would be used on healthy individuals considered useless or unable to work. Scholars disagree about exactly when gassing at Auschwitz became common practice for larger groups of prisoners. What is clear is that a technological breakthrough occurred in the summer of 1941.

The euthanasia program typically used carbon monoxide to kill victims. However, it was costly and required special equipment. Knowing this, Adolf Eichmann searched for an alternative that was more cost-effective and requested the SS commanders search as well. Karl Fritzsch, Höss's deputy, had the idea of using a different chemical cocktail, one that was readily available in large amounts.

Auschwitz had been built from the run-down and abandoned barracks of the Polish army. The barracks, crawling with lice, rats, and cockroaches, needed fumigation. For that purpose, camp guards used prussic acid, or hydrogen cyanide, a form of which was sold under the label Zyklon-Blausäure (Cyclone Cyanide). This Zyklon B, Fritzsch came to believe, could be used on Jews. Now Fritzsch had only to decide on a place to test the product.

As Auschwitz became a fully functioning camp in late 1940 and early 1941, few buildings were as frightening as Block 11. Part of the original camp building and built from red brick, Block 11 looked normal. However, word quickly spread that

Zyklon B canisters remain at Auschwitz, reminding visitors of the tragic death of thousands in the gas chambers.

THEY MADE HISTORY: IRENA SENDLER

Some people risked their lives to help Jews during World War II. Irena Sendler was one such hero. Several years after the Nazis invaded Poland on September 1, 1939—the start of the war in Europe—Sendler became one of the leaders of Zegota, an underground group founded partly to save children from the Warsaw ghetto in Poland.

A Roman Catholic by faith, Sendler and her volunteers did whatever they had to in order to smuggle the youngest and most fragile of the Polish Jews to safety. Children were placed in coffins and ambulances—anything to ferry them from certain death. At times, Jewish children were sent into church confessionals and given papers making them "Catholic." They would then be adopted by a Christian home or sent to an orphanage or convent.

Rather than recognizing herself as a hero, Irena Sendler credited the parents who were brave enough to trust their children to her and her colleagues in order to save their lives.

In 2007, after being honored by the Polish government, Sendler wrote, "Every child saved with my help and the help of all the wonderful secret messengers . . . is the justification of my existence on this earth, and not a title to glory."[1] Generations survive because of her efforts. Irena Sendler died in May 2008 at the age of 98.

1. Quoted in Dennis Hevesi, "Irena Sendler, Lifeline to Young Jews, Is Dead at 98," *New York Times*, May 13, 2008, www.nytimes.com/2008/05/13/world/europe/13sendler.html.

it was a place prisoners were sent to be tortured and killed. Block 11 appeared to be the perfect place to test this newly discovered method of mass slaughter. As the SS men worked to prepare the building, many prisoners understood the activity did not mean anything good. The Nazis experimented on ill prisoners and Russian prisoners of war. In one instance, the gas failed to work completely, and some of the inmates were left alive, only to die the next day.

Auschwitz Expansion

Heinrich Himmler visited Auschwitz for the first time at the end of 1940. He ordered that the camp be expanded from 10,000 to 30,000 prisoners, which would make it the largest Nazi concentration camp. In October 1941, construction of Auschwitz II, also called Auschwitz-Birkenau, began. The nearby village of Brzezinka, Poland (which was called Birkenau in German) was evacuated in order to provide space for the massive facility.

Auschwitz prisoners were tasked with building their new prison. In addition to Jews, Polish dissidents, Romani, and others, there were more than 10,000 Soviet prisoners of war (POWs). Apart from Jews, the Soviet Communists were the Nazis' most hated enemy. The completed camp was divided into 10 parts, which were separated by barbed-wire electric fences. Guard towers surrounded the camp, while inside there were about 300 barracks and buildings. Women and men were largely kept apart.

Each barracks held about 500 inmates, but overcrowding was not unusual. There were no windows in the barracks to protect from heat or cold. There were no bathrooms in them, either—just a bucket. It was unusual for prisoners to last more than a few weeks or months at Auschwitz-Birkenau. They were given little food, much of it spoiled. The terrible conditions, including the lack of clean water, allowed diseases such as smallpox and dysentery to spread easily. Those who did survive speak of extreme brutality—beatings, torture, starvation—that sometimes turned inmates against one another. According to some accounts, desperately hungry prisoners may have resorted to cannibalism.

The extremely crowded, cold, uncomfortable conditions of the barracks at Auschwitz are evident in this photograph from 1945, shortly after the camp was liberated.

Still, Auschwitz's days as a death camp had only started. In mid-1942, the construction of four huge gas chambers and crematoria began. The Germans estimated that more than 1.5 million people a year could be exterminated at the Auschwitz camp complex.

How You See History

1. Why is the diary of a young person like Anne Frank so important to the study of the Holocaust?
2. What is your reaction to the saying "Work makes one free," which is placed over the gate into Auschwitz?
3. How was the impetus for the T4 euthanasia program similar to the motivation for the Final Solution?

Strážní věž "SS"
Krematorium

CHAPTER THREE

LIVING AND DYING IN AUSCHWITZ

The Nazis were not the first or the last to attempt genocide. However, they were the most systematic, with their Final Solution including chillingly calculated methods of locating, transporting, and killing Jews. Those who were not immediately gassed at the death camps lived and labored in terrible conditions, until they were too weak to work and were then put to death.

No Jewish person was safe in any Nazi-held territory. Those who had been German citizens for generations suddenly found themselves herded onto overcrowded cattle trains and taken to concentration camps. To make them easier to control, the Nazis often lied to their prisoners, assuring them nothing bad would happen to them. Many believed their captors. Why? Hope was all they had left.

Running Out of Options

Escape was no longer possible for most Jews remaining in countries such as Germany, Poland, and Hungary, which had officially aligned itself with Germany by the end of 1940. Already herded into ghettos with little food or running water, many families—desperate and weary—could do nothing to change their fates. SS officials often demanded that local Jewish councils produce lists of people for deportation. Letters then went out ordering those listed to report to deportation centers. The Nazis did not reveal destinations, only

A train crowded with Hungarian Jews arrives in Auschwitz in 1944.

This map provides a closer look at major parts of Europe during World War II, including the sites of death camps.

saying that the Jews were being relocated to work farms in the east. Later, in an effort to speed up the process, SS squads went house to house, rounding up dozens of Jews at a time.

German citizens, with a few exceptions, encouraged this mass expulsion of its remaining Jewish population. Some of those detained had to wait days for transportation and were kept like caged animals behind barbed-wire fences with little to eat. Finally, boxcars made for cattle arrived for them.

Loading these "special" freight trains could take five or six hours. Travel time was hours or days. The cattle cars were so jammed with people that there was nowhere to sit, and people lacked food, water, and fresh air. Many victims died standing up. Those who did survive recall the torturous ride and the desperate urge to live, even under the harshest conditions imaginable. Ruth Kluger described her train ride to Auschwitz this way:

HISTORY HAPPENED HERE: THE UMSCHLAGPLATZ OF LODZ

The German word for the holding area where Jews and other prisoners were contained until they could be placed on trains was *umschlagplatz*, which means "concentration point." The Radogoszcz (or Radegast) Station was the umschlagplatz of Lodz, Poland. About 200,000 Jews passed through this station, forced out of the Litzmannstadt Ghetto of the city and taken to camps, including Auschwitz.

Today, the station, in addition to art installations there, serves as a monument to the dead. A wall separates the station from the rest of Lodz, a reminder of the isolation of the Jewish people of Europe under Hitler during the war. Visitors can walk through the structure called the "Tunnel of the Deported" at the station, a remembrance of the dark journey of the Nazis' victims. The walls of the tunnel are decorated with the names of those on the transport lists. Only an estimated 5 percent of the Jewish people of Lodz survived the war.

At the memorial at Radogoszcz Station, six gravestones bear the names of German concentration camps.

The doors were sealed, and air came through a small rectangle that served as [a] window … Only one person could stand in this privileged spot, and he was not likely to give it up … There were simply too many of us ... Soon the wagon reeked with the various smells that humans produce if they have to stay where they are ... It was summer, the temperature rose. The still air smelled of sweat, urine, excrement. A whiff of panic trembled in the air.[1]

At times, the cars were so crowded that those inside suffocated before their arrival at the death camps.

From People to Prisoners

Prisoners who survived the trip arrived at Auschwitz weak, frightened, and desperate for water. Without warning, they would hear the sounds of a large gate clanging open. The train suddenly stopped, and the boxcar doors flew open. Police dogs barked; people screamed. Squads of workers separated them from their luggage and other possessions, which they were told would be returned to them. The arrivals were herded along "the ramp," the long strip of pavement next to the railway where chaos was deliberately designed to intimidate the arrivals.

Beginning in 1943, camp doctor Josef Mengele stood on the ramp as prisoners were unloaded and paraded past him. He eyed each one carefully, assessing vitality and strength, ability to work, and specific characteristics that might qualify an arrival for medical experimentation. Quickly, he pointed at each person to step to the right or left. His decision meant life or death. Roughly 10 percent of new arrivals, the ones directed to step to the right—mostly men and teenage boys—were sent off to work. The other 90 percent—primarily women and children, directed to step to the left—were sent directly to the gas chambers.

Prisoners who survived were formally processed in a series of dehumanizing steps. First, they were told to strip off their clothes and put them on hooks behind them, with their shoes on the floor underneath. At the next station, barbers shaved all the hair off their heads and bodies. Smaller prisoners were made to stand on stools. To make extra money, the Nazis sold the hair to manufacturing companies for such uses as stuffing mattresses and making rope. Once all their hair was gone, prisoners were tattooed with numbers so the guards

Auschwitz survivor Sam Beller shows his prisoner number tattoo as he visits the former concentration camp in 2015.

could easily identify them. Auschwitz was the only camp that tattooed its inmates.

Clothing came next: a striped shirt and pants or smock-type dress, jacket, cap, and wooden clogs for shoes. Prisoners received no underwear. After getting their clothes, they were handed two strips of cloth with the Star of David and the tattooed number on them. These cloths were sewn onto the uniform. Finally, prisoners were given a small, round bowl for daily rations. This bowl became their lifeline.

Women and men were then separately forced into disinfecting showers. Former prisoner Cecilie Klein-Pollack remembers being forced into these showers soon after her arrival, shorn of her hair and frightened. She said, "They first opened the hot water, so we were scalded and as we ran out from under the hot water, we were beaten back by the SS and by the Kapos to go under the showers again, so they opened the ice cold water, which had the same effect."[2]

PAST MEETS PRESENT: REMEMBERING THE HOLOCAUST THROUGH LITERATURE AND FILM

Hundreds of books and movies have been created—and are still being produced—that center on the horrors of the Holocaust. Some are nonfiction, such as *Anne Frank: The Diary of a Young Girl*; *Night* by Elie Wiesel; and the graphic novel *Maus* by Art Spiegelman. Others are historical fiction, keeping the facts of the Holocaust but creating a fictional story. These include *The Pianist*, *Everything Is Illuminated*, *The Book Thief*, and many others.

While reading fictional accounts can be helpful in grasping the basic history of the Holocaust, reading primary source accounts of the Holocaust is vital. Only the people who were there can accurately describe the emotional and physical impact of this tragic period. Still, it is important for contemporary writers, researchers, and filmmakers to continue producing Holocaust literature and films, fiction and nonfiction, because it is critical for people today and future generations to remember what happened. When survivors speak about the Holocaust, they say, "Never forget. Never again."

While new arrivals were initiated into the camp system, slave laborers pored over the valuables of those just stripped of all their belongings. In Auschwitz, innocent people lost not only their freedom but their possessions. They were now utterly at the mercy of the Third Reich.

"Annihilation Through Labor"

Selection for work was only a temporary reprieve from death, and the kind of labor Auschwitz inmates were subjected to was often horrific. Hours were long, the work itself nearly unbearable. This "annihilation through labor" destroyed the bodies and the wills of hundreds of thousands of camp prisoners, who were forced to

Elie Wiesel, author and winner of the Nobel Peace Prize, is seen in this photograph inside a barracks at Buchenwald concentration camp in Germany. He is seventh from the left on the middle of the three main bunks, next to the post.

survive on meager rations and little water. If a prisoner broke down or was unable to work, the SS guard sent him to the gas chambers. Auschwitz prisoners were likely, then, to die either way. However, before they did, their work earned profits for the Nazi state and its allies. In late 1940, Nazi-connected businesses began taking advantage of all the cheap labor the party was making available to them. Himmler and other Nazi officials, determined to exploit their captive populations for industrial labor to support the war effort, encouraged chemical corporation IG Farben and other industrialists to build plants near the death camps.

Auschwitz III, also known as Buna or Monowitz, opened in October 1942. It primarily housed prisoners who worked at IG Farben's synthetic rubber works plant, located near the Polish town of Monowice. The company constructed the factory in the town for the express purpose of using laborers from the camp and making a profit. IG Farben invested heavily in the project and agreed to pay for the use of the forced labor. Forty-four other subcamps were put into use near the Auschwitz complex between 1942 and 1944. These served various businesses. The smaller facilities included coal mines, stone quarries, and armament factories that supplied the German military.

Other work consisted of burying the bodies of the dead. In the camp's early months, Commandant Höss struggled over what to do with thousands of rotting corpses. Initially, they were buried in a field, but the holes were not deep enough and the summer heat made the smell of rotting flesh unbearable. Auschwitz survivor Otto Pressburger remembered:

> *We had to dig the bodies out and burn them. A big fire was made here with wood and petrol and we were throwing them right into it. There were always two of us throwing the bodies in—one holding the legs and one on the arms. The smell and the stench was terrible. The bodies were not only bloody but rotten as well.*[3]

The Angel of Death

Not all of those saved from immediate extermination at Auschwitz were put to work. At Dr. Mengele's direction, identical twins and people with genetic abnormalities such as dwarfism were often taken aside and told to see camp doctors for better treatment. Parents of children in these categories readily agreed to what they believed would be special care. Adults in these categories sometimes volunteered themselves, assuming they too would be spared the miserable conditions of the slave laborers.

These new patients kept their civilian clothes and stayed in barracks far cleaner and more accommodating than those in the other parts of the camp. The food here tasted good, and there was plenty of it. Before long, the medical exams began. Patients had their blood taken, their ears checked, and their blood pressure gauged. The camp artist, a Jewish woman named Dina Gottliebova, painted

THEY MADE HISTORY: DINA GOTTLIEBOVA

Annemarie Dinah "Dina" Gottliebova was born in Brno, Czechoslovakia, on January 21, 1923. Germany invaded Czechoslovakia in 1939, changing her life forever. She and her mother, Johanna Gottlieb, arrived at Auschwitz in 1943. Once an art student, Dina's talent was apparent after she painted pictures on the walls of a barracks for children. She painted animals as well as characters from the movie *Snow White and the Seven Dwarfs*. Camp doctor Josef Mengele heard about her art and wanted her to work for him, documenting his experiments on Auschwitz's inmates. Dina told him she would walk into the camp's electrified fence if he did not save her mother's life too. Mengele agreed.

Following the war, Dina and her mother moved to Paris, France. After she married Art Babbitt, the couple immigrated to the United States, where she worked on movies, cartoons, and other projects. Some of her watercolor portraits from Auschwitz were eventually found and acquired by the Auschwitz-Birkenau Memorial and State Museum, though Dina endeavored to get them back for the rest of her life. She died in 2009, never achieving that goal. However, a Marvel comic strip of her story was created and later adapted into the short film "The Last Outrage."

many of them for the camp's records. Mengele insisted on the paintings because he wanted accurate representations of Romani prisoners' skin tone. This was hard to capture on camera at that time. Gottliebova agreed to do it in exchange for a guarantee of safety for herself and her mother.

As a medical officer and SS captain, Mengele earned a stellar reputation among his superiors in the Third Reich, and on May 30, 1943, he arrived at Auschwitz as the camp's chief doctor. Doctors are trained to aid humankind: study patients, determine ailments,

Dr. Josef Mengele's experiments on twins may have been "research" into how to double the birth rate for the so-called Aryan race.

and suggest treatments. However, in the disordered world of Auschwitz, Mengele and the doctors on his staff made "patients" ill intentionally to observe how their already fragile bodies responded to pain, disease, and physical torment.

Because of his unique set of interests, Mengele's experiments were often different than those performed elsewhere. At places such as Buchenwald concentration camp, Nazi doctors injected prisoners with diseases such as typhus, smallpox, or yellow fever to take note of how their bodies responded. Historian Gretchen Engle Schafft wrote about the difference between Mengele's placid exterior and his merciless cruelty: "He moved in an elegant fashion, always carefully dressed in uniform … A kindergarten was set up, and the children received special rations. They routinely called him 'Uncle' or even 'Papa.' This behavior stood in stark contrast to his absolutely emotionless approach to experiments."[4]

Nazi ideology was founded upon the principle that northern Europeans were superior to other people. Mengele's ghoulish experiments existed to support his belief in "race science," including the idea that Jews were genetically inferior. Mengele chose twins for many sadistic, unethical experiments. He wanted to show that physically changing one twin by brutal medical procedures could not change that person's genetic makeup compared with the other twin. Mengele's obsession with twins led to his attempts to change their eye color with chemicals and surgically change fraternal twins into Siamese twins.

Doctor Miklós Nyiszli, a prisoner forced to work for Mengele, autopsied Mengele's victims on a regular basis. He hoped that his work for the Nazi doctor would spare the lives of his wife and daughter. Nyiszli discovered Mengele's horrific work. Victims already sick or made sick by the doctors in the camp "infirmary" were rarely treated except by an injection of chloroform to the heart.

During his tenure at Auschwitz, Mengele sickened, disfigured, or killed more than 3,000 pairs of twins. His reputation at Auschwitz earned him the ominous nickname "Angel of Death."

Another Method of Killing

Prisoners died in many ways at Auschwitz, including shooting, starvation, and disease. However, these methods involved uncertainty: Death did not always fit a timetable, and the system was therefore not efficient. The Nazis' preferred method of killing—the gas chamber—left nothing to chance and sped up the killing process.

Although the first Zyklon B tests were done at Auschwitz I, Auschwitz-Birkenau quickly became the primary killing center. In late February 1942, Höss ordered a planned body disposal center, or crematorium, to move from Auschwitz I to Auschwitz-Birkenau. At the same time, Höss and other officials decided to use an old farmer's cottage on the grounds as a makeshift gas chamber. Known as "the Little Red House," or Bunker 1, the cottage earned its name after workers bricked up all of its windows and doors. The house's inner walls, kitchen, and other areas were removed and replaced with two new sealed spaces. Different entryways were also created, as was a small hatch near the top of the brickwork for the Zyklon B pellets.

"The Little Red House" became Auschwitz-Birkenau's first fully functioning gas chamber. Only weeks later, a second site, "the Little White House" or Bunker 2, went into operation. The rooms in Bunker 2 were smaller and narrower, but it had four of them, and the ventilation was better. Twelve hundred people at one time could be gassed there.

The Nazis told prisoners who were sent straight to the gas chambers upon arrival that they would be taking a shower. The victims were first shown into a room and then told to remove their clothes

A visitor examines one of the gas chambers at Auschwitz-Birkenau. Most victims thought—and were told—that the facilities were showers.

and hang them on hooks. As inmates undressed, SS often encouraged them to remember which hook was theirs and to hurry so they would not be too late to enjoy the hot coffee that awaited them after their warm shower. However, once they were ushered into the "showers," the prisoners knew that something was wrong. The women were led in first, followed by men, and then children were forced into any empty space. The more people that were packed into the room, the sooner they suffocated. In 15 to 20 minutes, it was all over. During the height of the deportations of Hungarian Jews in 1944, about 6,000 died this way daily at Auschwitz-Birkenau.

Crematoria

Auschwitz's reputation as a notorious death camp only grew—and became a source of pride for the Third Reich. Historian Laurence Rees stated, "It was obvious to men like Himmler that the only installation in the Nazi empire capable of satisfactorily uniting the twin goals of work and murder was Auschwitz."[5]

This reliance on Auschwitz's role in the Final Solution meant more prisoners were shipped there. The numbers of dead swelled

FROM THE SOURCE: SAM ITZKOWITZ DESCRIBES DEATH BY GAS CHAMBER

Years later, prisoner Sam Itzkowitz recalled the gas chambers at Auschwitz well, in part because he helped build them:

Sometimes they had 20 or 30 extra people that they couldn't get in, so they always held back children ... they made the kids crawl on top of the heads, all the way in there, just kept on pushing them in, to fill them all in ... [then] the door was slammed behind them, [it] was a thick door, was about six inches thick ... The men, the SS men were standing outside with a Red Cross wagon and they had the gas can ... in the ambulance. He put a mask on, had to put a mask on, tore the lid off of the gas ... threw it down the chute, through the chimney into the gas chamber. The crematorium two and three had two gas chutes. And as soon as he threw the gas in, he slammed the lid shut, so the gas wouldn't escape. And all you could hear is one loud sound, "Shema ..." [the Jewish declaration of faith] and that was all.[1]

1. Sam Itzkowitz, "Sam Itzkowitz Describes Gas Chambers in Auschwitz," United States Holocaust Memorial Museum, www.ushmm.org/wlc/en/media_oi.php?ModuleId=0&MediaId=1217 (accessed January 12, 2021).

to such a degree that the disposal of bodies became a major concern to Höss and other Auschwitz officials. Cremation was chosen as the most efficient method of dealing with the dead, and the large numbers of dead demanded more than one crematorium.

The first crematorium operated from August 1940 until July 1943. According to German authorities, 340 corpses could be burned every 24 hours in the facility's three furnaces. Still, this proved not to be enough for the camp's death rate, particularly when an influx of prisoners arrived. By spring 1943, Auschwitz-Birkenau

The museum that now exists at Auschwitz rebuilt this destroyed crematorium so visitors could understand the true history of the camp complex.

featured four crematoria. They had eight gas chambers and 46 ovens that burned about 4,400 corpses each day.

As with other operations in the camp, prisoners were selected to form groups to take bodies from the gas chambers to the crematoria. These units were called Sonderkommandos, or "special command units." The Sonderkommandos carted the bodies from the chambers. Then, prisoners were ordered to use pliers and other tools to extract gold fillings from the victims' teeth and toss the teeth into a bucket of acid. The gold was used to enrich Nazi treasuries.

The victims were then loaded into the ovens, which sometimes ran 24 hours a day. Cremation took about 20 minutes. The fumes of burning flesh and dark smoke served as constant reminders of the furnaces' purpose. Sonderkommandos dumped the ashes of the dead into the nearby Vistula River.

Despite the number of crematoria at work, sometimes they were not enough to keep up with the numbers of dead. This happened in

1944, when more than 380,000 Hungarian Jews were transported to Auschwitz-Birkenau, where most would die. German authorities ordered that their bodies be burned and thrown into pits behind the crematorium known as Crematorium V.

By this point in the war, German command knew the war was turning against the Third Reich. This knowledge only caused those obsessed with the Final Solution to speed up the killing process.

Many who survived Auschwitz-Birkenau marvel that they did. Some speak of their will to live, a stranger's kindness, or sheer luck that saved them while so many others could not be saved.

How You See History

1. How did German businesses play a role in the growth of Auschwitz?
2. Why was it important to camp officials to keep the gas chambers a secret from the prisoners?
3. Why do you think prisoners were forced to do the duties of the Sonderkommandos and not German soldiers?

CHAPTER FOUR

THE SURVIVORS

Auschwitz was a place of death. Everything was designed to ultimately kill those imprisoned within its confines, swiftly or slowly. Hard labor, lack of food and water, appalling living conditions, the brutality of the guards, and finally, the gas chambers all worked together to tell the inmates to surrender all hope. Incredibly, though, some did not give up. Their sheer will to live helped them survive.

Many credit their fellow prisoners for saving their lives, some of whom did not survive themselves. The kindness of these people, no matter how small, provided comfort to carry others through. For example, 17-year-old Henia Bryer, who spent three months in Auschwitz, recalled weeping because she knew she would die in the freezing temperatures: "I stood there and cried. I thought, 'I don't know how to survive in these clothes.' I was standing in the snow in a micro-mini dress with nothing on my head."[1] Luckily, another inmate, who had been a worker at the shoe factory owned by Bryer's father, threw her clothes that fit, clothes that had been collected from the dead. These garments likely saved the teenager's life, helping her survive until the camp was evacuated a few months later.

In fact, many survivors credit luck, a miracle, or mere chance to their survival. Certainly, Bryer's warmer clothes might have gone to

This display of shoes at Auschwitz reminds visitors of the tragic numbers of people who were killed—or worked to death—at the concentration camp. Their belongings were stripped from the bodies.

someone else if the giver had not recognized her. Most Auschwitz survivors still marvel that they lived while others did not.

Desperate Choices

As prisoners' bodies withered, so did their normal sense of right and wrong. Stealing among the population was common, and betrayal of fellow prisoners was as well. Collaboration with the SS and other camp guards could mean the difference between a longer life and immediate execution.

While many inmates considered Sonderkommandos to be traitors for their part in burning bodies and working in the Auschwitz "infirmary," the squad members themselves had struck a bargain they hoped would delay their own extermination. In return for their participation, they ate better food, were housed in livable barracks, and wore civilian clothes. They also had access to Nazi commanders that many others did not have.

When prisoner Miklós Nyiszli realized that his wife and daughter would soon be gassed, he bribed an SS officer to have his family transferred to a women's work unit. Still, he, like the Sonderkommando members, knew that after a few months in the service of his jailers, he would also be gassed and burned.

Holocaust survivor Miriam Ziegler shows a picture of herself and other prisoners in Auschwitz. Many could not speak of the horrors they experienced for many years.

In desperate times, humans look for ways to survive, even temporarily. Their methods and morals may differ, but in the harshness of Auschwitz, prisoners were often forced to make choices they never imagined they would have to.

Other prisoners resisted any threat to their sense of humanity or morality. Auschwitz survivor Primo Levi wrote extensively about his Holocaust experience. In one noted passage in his best-known work, *If This Is a Man* (also titled *Survival in Auschwitz*), Levi, an Italian chemist sent to Auschwitz in February 1944, remembers arguing with a fellow inmate about hygiene. What was the purpose of washing yourself, Levi had asked, when you were about to die? The other prisoner, Steinlauf, told him that because the Nazis' goal was to dehumanize them, it was their job to resist as much as possible and not give in, either to the Nazis or to the temptation to degrade themselves: "We must not become beasts … even in this place one can survive, and therefore one must want to survive, to tell the story, to bear witness … We are slaves, deprived of every right, exposed to every insult, condemned to certain death, but we still possess one power … the power to refuse our consent."[2]

On the Brink of Death

By 1943, Nazi Germany's ambition had clearly outstripped its ability to fight a war on numerous fronts. Inmates of the camp longed to hear any word that the Third Reich could be defeated. However, Auschwitz remained a world within the world—an inferno of pain, misery, and sickness without light, joy, or, seemingly, a road out. Often alone, separated from their families, prisoners at Auschwitz looked for a way—any way—to survive just one more day.

The long, wooden barracks in which inmates lived did not make survival easy. Bunk beds made from boards slept five or six people each, so tightly packed that if one person turned, everyone had to turn. A narrow brick stove ran the length of the barracks between the bunks. There were no blankets, nothing to bring comfort to the cold and weary.

The toilets were little more than large outhouses, and prisoners had to clean them out with shovels when they were filled. There was no toilet paper. However, prisoners wanted to work there because camp officers never entered the latrines. The inmates could discuss escape plans or trade cigarettes or food. Plus, latrine workers also stank so badly from their jobs that the guards often left them alone.

At or before dawn each day, a loud bell woke camp workers, and guards drove their captives out of the barracks for roll call. Those who had died during the night lay in their beds or on the ground, soon to be carted to the crematoria. Before roll call, prisoners had to

The Nazis had little reason to make the barracks of their concentration camps more comfortable, or even livable. They did not care if the inhabitants died.

exercise regardless of how sick or feeble they were or how cold or hot it was outside.

The roll call itself could last hours, and prisoners sometimes died during it. Those who survived long enough for their breakfast ration received some bread with a bit of salami or margarine and weak coffee. Survivor Heniek Sztarkman said, "Food was always a problem. Always. You were constantly hungry. Later on, as conditions became worse towards the end, there were sometimes periods of three days when there was no food to be had at all."[3]

After a 10- to 11-hour day at work in the camps, prisoners returned to a dinner of watery soup. The poor diets and the lack of sanitary conditions at Auschwitz meant disease was endemic. Ironically,

At the end of 1943, barracks were set up at Auschwitz for children older than two years old. Children did not receive better treatment than adult prisoners, however.

the SS often wrote reminders on barracks rafters, including *Sauberkeit ist Gesundheit*, or "Cleanliness is Health." These words were cruel because the prisoners were not given regular showers, so they were unable to stay clean. Lice infested the inmates' bodies. Rats and bedbugs also had to be dealt with.

Such unsanitary conditions bred sickness. Common—and often deadly—ailments included typhus and dysentery. Most prisoners suffered from diarrhea. Although the numbers of people who died from disease alone at Auschwitz are uncertain, a large percentage of deaths were caused by something other than gassing, often during the night. In the morning, inmates would often awake to find their bunkmate dead or near death.

Working in "Canada"

An ongoing task in the operations at Auschwitz took place in a section of Auschwitz-Birkenau known as "Canada," a large warehouse where inmate workers sorted through victims' pants, jackets, briefcases, and underwear looking for money, diamonds, and anything else of significance. It was called "Canada" because the actual country of Canada was thought to be a nation of wealth. When one of the workers found something of worth, they slipped it into a wooden box; it now belonged to the Reich. Heaps of possessions—coats, socks,

THEY MADE HISTORY: RAPHAEL LEMKIN

The term "genocide"—the deliberate killing of people who belong to a certain racial, ethnic, political, or religious group—was first coined by a young Jewish lawyer who fled the Nazi assault on Poland: Raphael Lemkin. In 1944, he created the term by combining *genos*, the Greek word for "race," with the suffix *-cide*, which comes from a Latin word meaning "to kill."

Born into a Polish-Jewish family in what is now Lithuania in 1900, Lemkin took an early interest in the fates of cultures, especially the undeclared Armenian genocide by the Turks in the years before World War I. He later wrote how, from a young age, he "was appalled by the frequency of evil ... and, above all, by the impunity coldly relied upon by the guilty."[1]

After earning his law degree, Lemkin worked as the public prosecutor in Warsaw, Poland, from 1929 to 1934. There he helped rewrite and redefine the Polish penal code and lectured before the League of Nations on criminal law. In 1939, he saw action in the Polish army and defended the country against the Nazi onslaught. He arrived in the United States in 1941. Forty-nine of his family members who could not escape died in the Holocaust. Lemkin's best-known book, *Axis Rule in Occupied Europe*, argues for international laws against genocide. He spent the rest of his life trying to get such laws passed. In 1948, the United Nations approved the Convention on the Prevention and Punishment of Genocide. Lemkin died in 1959.

Raphael Lemkin's critical work was not lauded in his own time, though he is much respected today.

1. Quoted in Samantha Power, *"A Problem from Hell": America and the Age of Genocide* (New York, NY: Basic Books, 2013), p. 20.

and hats—were then sent to the Reich Economic Ministry or the Ethnic German Liaison Office. Many workers in "Canada" considered themselves lucky, as they were better fed than those in other parts of the camp. Thievery became common, as both workers and the SS smuggled items out of the building.

Stolen valuables and cash became such an issue in the camp that by October 1943, Himmler drew a distinction between what he considered justifiable crime and the crime of stealing. Riches diverted and crimes committed to support the Nazi state were acceptable, but individual theft for personal gain was unacceptable, dishonorable, and harshly punished. According to Laurence Rees, "for them [the Nazis] to be able to live with themselves … he had to paint a picture of the SS members as killers of women and children, yes, but murderers who had still retained their honor."[4]

Use and Abuse of Prisoners

Most members of the Third Reich, including the charming Dr. Mengele, thought any relationship between a "racially superior" Nazi and a "lowly" Jew was an abomination. However, the connections between the prisoners and their captors were complex at times. In rare cases, Nazis and their family members showed signs of compassion for the suffering people, at least recognizing them as human beings. (Officers at Auschwitz typically lived there with their families.) The following story reveals the complexity of camp life for some captives.

Józef Paczyński, a camp barber, was bunkmates with Stanislaw Dubiel, who worked at Rudolf Höss's home as a gardener. Paczyński had long desired tomatoes from the commandant's vegetable garden, which sat not far from one of the crematoria. After his friend Dubiel showed him the best way to reach the tomatoes, Paczyński stole them from the garden. On the way out, he ran into Höss's wife and was certain he would be killed for his infraction. Later, Dubiel told Paczyński that he had taken the blame for the theft. Dubiel and Frau Höss knew one another, and he was valuable to her. She saw nothing wrong with him taking some vegetables, and the matter was forgotten. This kind of experience was the key to survival for many inmates—if the Nazis considered you to be useful, you lived, at least for a while.

The power imbalance between guards and women prisoners especially led to incidents of sexual abuse. Some camps even created brothels where women were forced to work. Any woman who became pregnant was forced to have an abortion or, if she could hide the pregnancy, give birth in secret.

Even the so-called family camp of the Birkenau section, created in September 1943, fell victim to the whims and depravity of the Nazi SS. The camp contained 18,000 people deported from the Theresienstadt ghetto in Czechoslovakia. The Nazis intended to use these prisoners, separated from other inmates by barbed-wire fences, as positive propaganda. "Family camp" captives were ordered to write letters home telling family and friends that, despite the rumors, they were being treated well by the Nazis. Still, women in this part of the camp were vulnerable to attacks by SS guards too.

Daring to Escape

With its tight security and barbed-wire fencing, Auschwitz made escape seem foolhardy—but it was not impossible. Earlier, since most of the prisoners were Poles, there was a chance that fugitives could actually get away. Civilians in the Polish countryside surrounding Auschwitz were likely to be sympathetic to the inmates' trouble. Escapees might blend in with the locals if they could get past the perimeter fence. In the camp's first year of operation, only one known escape was attempted. Dressed as a civilian worker, a Pole named Tadeusz Wiejowski walked out with the civilian workers. Prevention came by way of example; those who tried to escape and were caught were tortured. Five civilian workers were incarcerated for helping Wiejowski, for example. Prisoners' families or block mates would bear the burden of the punishment if the escaping prisoners were not caught.

One high-profile escape occurred in 1942. Planned by Polish political prisoner Kazimierz Piechowski and spurred on by the scheduled execution of his friend, the idea called for obtaining a set of SS uniforms. However, neither Piechowski nor his co-conspirators could figure out how to get them. Then, a stroke of luck: a Kapo told Piechowski to retrieve boxes from one of the rooms in the warehouse in which he worked. While looking for them, he came across a room marked "Uniforms."

Days later, Piechowski found the door slightly ajar. He pushed the door open but found an SS man working inside. He received a beating from the guard and was ordered to report to the main office.

FROM THE SOURCE: JÓZEF PACZYŃSKI

Józef Paczyński, an inmate who arrived at Auschwitz in 1940, was lucky enough to make a life for himself as a barber for the SS staff. Unlike most, Paczyński came in close contact with Commandant Rudolf Höss and at least once visited his house to give him a trim. Paczyński marveled at the power he had over the camp's highest official at that moment:

> *Höss came in and sat down. I stood at attention. He had a cigar in his mouth and was reading a paper. I did the same haircut I had seen done on him before. Höss didn't say a word to me, and I didn't say a word. I was afraid, and he despised inmates. I had a razor in my hand. I could have cut his throat … But I'm a thinking being, and you know what would have happened? My whole family would have been destroyed … In his place someone else would have come.*[1]

1. Quoted in Laurence Rees, *Auschwitz: A New History* (New York, NY: Public Affairs), p. 84.

Knowing that if he did as he was told he would be killed, Piechowski did nothing and hoped the Nazi guard would forget about the incident, which he did.

On June 20, 1942, a day off for SS men in the warehouse, Piechowski and his small crew, including his friend, took a chance. They put on stolen SS uniforms and took four machine guns and eight hand grenades from a storage area. They hopped into a car another member of the group had acquired and drove toward the main gate. Along the way, they played the part of loyal soldiers, raising their arms and shouting "Heil Hitler" as SS men rolled by. They had no documents to support their roles as Nazis; they hoped they would not need them.

They drove slowly toward the gate, but it did not open as they got closer. Piechowski revealed he considered killing himself. Instead, not wanting to let the others down, "I yelled at the SS [men]: 'How long are we going to be waiting here!' I cursed them. And then the SS man at

PAST MEETS PRESENT: EVER-PRESENT PREJUDICE

The extreme prejudice the Nazis had for the Jews is still shocking today. However, racism and prejudice have always been used as tools to create scapegoats for people's problems. Throughout all of history, lies have been spread about various peoples in order to turn others against them. During the Holocaust, posters were put up in German cities showing Jews with horns—implying that they were children of the devil—and stating that they were dirty, diseased, corrupt, and more. In the United States during the same time period, anti-Japanese feelings grew strong after the bombing of Pearl Harbor. Posters and ads showed Japanese people with fangs and claws, along with statements implying that even American-born Japanese citizens were spies and encouraging people to be suspicious of them.

Such prejudice still exists. Some prejudiced propaganda is aimed at Muslims, for example. The people who create this misinformation use the threat of violence from radical Islamic groups such as ISIS to fuel their misleading ideas, suggesting that people should fear all Muslims and ignoring the fact that the vast majority of Muslims have publicly condemned radical groups. In the United States, the political opponents of former U.S. president Barack Obama claimed that he was secretly a Muslim, an attempt to persuade voters to be afraid of supporting him. In addition, prejudice against immigrants from Latin American countries led some in the United States to turn a blind eye to their treatment at crowded facilities along the U.S. border with Mexico. In fact, some politicians and journalists referred to those facilities as concentration camps.

the watchtower said something and he opened the gate and we went through. That was freedom."[5] Outside the dreaded gates of Auschwitz, the four drove through the Polish countryside to a place where friends helped them get rid of their Nazi uniforms and the stolen car. The men soon blended in with the local population until the war was over.

Such daring escapes were rare but not unheard of. Less common, though, were outright rebellions. The SS kept tight control over their charges, and with the Sonderkommandos working for them, uprisings within Auschwitz were extraordinarily difficult to pull off.

As in many oppressive situations, though, an underground resistance to the camp system developed at Auschwitz. Highly secretive, it aimed to undermine Nazi power and free as many inmates as possible. A noted attempt at rebellion was led by Sonderkommando inmates in 1944.

The Nazis typically murdered their prison helpers after only a few months of work as a way of ensuring the secrecy of the gas chambers. However, as hope for Nazi victory in the war diminished and the likelihood that advancing Russian armies would liberate the Polish camps increased, Sonderkommandos realized that, like their fellow prisoners, death could come for them at any time. This compelled the 12th Sonderkommando group to act. Female prisoners had smuggled them gunpowder for months, which the men planned to use to destroy the crematoria and gas chambers. They also gathered knives and axes.

On October 7, 1944, the Polish and Hungarian Sonderkommandos in Crematorium IV attacked SS men with axes and rocks. Then, they blew up the crematorium and gas chamber. The Sonderkommandos in another crematorium saw the flames and determined the uprising had

A guard station towers over the electric fence of Auschwitz-Birkenau, a reminder of the tight security that daunted would-be escapees.

HISTORY HAPPENED HERE: THE AROLSEN ARCHIVES

The records of more than 17 million people incarcerated by the Nazis can be found in the Arolsen Archives–International Center on Nazi Persecution in the German town of Bad Arolsen. In 2007, the 16 miles (26 km) of shelves, containing more than 30 million documents, were opened to the public for the first time. Here, visitors can peruse arrest warrants and personal documents that paint a detailed picture of life under Nazi rule.

The archives were founded by the Allies after World War II as a place where people could find information on lost loved ones. It was then called the International Tracing Service. To make it easier for descendants, researchers, students, and others to access the collection, the Arolsen Archives began digitizing its collection in the 1980s. By 2020, about 26 million scanned documents had been posted online.

However, the archives do not have information on all Holocaust victims. For example, they do not have the names of those who were murdered immediately upon entering a concentration camp, those who were murdered by the Einsatzgruppen death squads, those who died in death marches, and those who were hidden during the war.

begun. They grabbed one SS guard, wrestled him into an oven, and burned him alive.

Before other prisoners could join the rebellion, Nazi guards fought back and brutally suppressed what became known as the largest revolt in the camp's history. About 250 prisoners were killed. After, about 200 Sonderkommando inmates and co-conspirators were captured and told to lie face down outside the crematoria, where they each received one bullet to the back of the head. The women who helped them obtain the gunpowder were hanged.

Family Matters

Some prisoners in Auschwitz would not even think of leaving because their family was in the camp complex too. They could not leave loved ones behind. Rather than this being a burden, having family members in camp was the connection they needed to survive. Spending time with a family member and helping them survive became the selfless focus they needed to keep going day after day. Fifteen-year-old Alice Lok (later, Cahana) never tried to escape. She channeled her energy into remaining close to her older sister, Edith.

In 1944, Edith came down with typhoid fever. The camp hospital was usually off limits to other prisoners, but young Alice found the courage to bribe a Kapo with bread. In exchange for visiting her sister, she even helped him carry dead bodies. Alice became a source of hope for the sick prisoners, inventing stories about the war's end and the freedom they all would have soon. However, Alice soon realized sick prisoners were sent to the gas chambers. Quickly, she devised a plan to save Edith from that fate.

Instructing Edith to "play dead," Alice carried her from the hospital, as she had done with other bodies. However, it became difficult to hide the ailing Edith among the healthy women. In October 1944, the two girls were selected for the gas chamber. Incredibly, the gas chamber malfunctioned, and the women were saved. Later, Alice and Edith were evacuated by the Nazis to the Bergen-Belsen camp as the Allied forces closed in. After they were liberated, Edith was taken to a Red Cross hospital. Sadly, Alice never saw her again. However, her link to her sister gave them both their best chance of survival.

Such heroic devotion did not have happy endings for most Auschwitz inmates. However, deliverance for the prisoners was close at hand by the fall of 1944—if they could only stay alive.

How You See History

1. Do you notice any similarities among the survivors in this chapter? Explain.
2. Why might Höss's wife have accepted her gardener, Stanislaw Dubiel, taking tomatoes but not the barber, Józef Paczyński?
3. How do you think other prisoners responded to the Sonderkommando revolt of 1944 and its aftermath?

CHAPTER FIVE

LIBERATION

By 1944, the once-mighty Third Reich was in retreat. It could no longer fight effectively on multiple fronts, and the additional forces of the United States and the Soviet Union had helped turn the tide of the war in favor of the Allies. While the Final Solution had been kept confidential for as long as possible from those outside Germany, it was impossible to keep such wide-scale killing a secret for long.

In 1942, journalists who had been released from German custody told the world what their Nazi sources had relayed about the extermination of Jewish communities. Still, people were not sure about the extent of the violence against Jews and other so-called enemies of the German state. However, on December 13, 1942, Edward R. Murrow of the CBS radio network reported, "Millions of human beings, most of them Jews, are being gathered up with ruthless efficiency and murdered. The phrase 'concentration camps' is obsolete … It is now possible only to speak of extermination camps."[1]

As the Allies drew closer to German-held territory in late 1944 and early 1945, the Nazis were instructed to destroy the camps and to remove the survivors to camps within German borders. Besides needing the prisoners for labor, the Nazis wanted to conceal the evidence of their crimes. In January 1945, Himmler ordered the

German civilians walk past the bodies of Jewish women who died of exhaustion during a forced march near the end of the war.

evacuation of all eastern camps, telling the camp commanders to not allow prisoners to fall into the hands of the Allies. This included the Auschwitz camp complex.

Eliminating All Evidence

On January 18, 1945, as the Soviet army approached, Auschwitz SS gathered close to 60,000 inmates in the wind and snow and told them to walk. Such infamous death marches took Nazi captors and their prisoners west into Germany. The plan was to kill as many as possible along the way and put any survivors into labor camps in Germany to continue the war effort. One group headed northwest to Gliwice, the other due west toward the Polish town of Wodzislaw. Prisoners who survived the journey often remember this portion of their Auschwitz experience as the worst ordeal of their captivity. The prisoners were already starved and weak. Many had no strength left for a forced march through rough terrain during the winter.

The SS tried to maintain order, but most prisoners could not keep the pace, falling from lack of food and water. "They took them through the woods and they marched at night," said Benjamin Ferencz, a soldier who helped liberate the camps. "And if anybody faltered on the way they were immediately shot; if anybody paused to try to pick up a potato or to eat a root or something, they were shot."[2] Ferencz later followed the trail of bodies for miles. An estimated 15,000 prisoners from Auschwitz died in the marches altogether.

Some of the prisoners helped each other because they had become friends or could not face being cruel. Gerda Weissmann Klein, who survived one of the death marches, recalled a moment when someone in a town the marchers passed through tossed her some bread. She saw the hands of many of her fellow marchers begging her to share. Though she wavered for a moment because she was so hungry, she decided to divide it. However, some prisoners stole food, shoes, and other tools of survival. The horrors they endured challenged them to make unimaginable decisions.

Prisoners who survived the marches were put on cargo trains bound for camps inside Germany. All across eastern Europe and throughout the network of Nazi concentration and death camps, similar scenes were being carried out.

THEY MADE HISTORY: GERDA WEISSMANN KLEIN

Gerda Weissmann was born May 8, 1924, in Bielsko, Poland. After the Nazis invaded Poland, her family was torn apart. Her older brother was forced to sign up for the German army but was never seen again. She was separated from her parents and sent to several camps. Her parents later died. Weissmann credited her father with saving her life. He made her wear boots when she was sent away, even though it was summer. Later, when she was on a death march during the winter of 1945, she was one of just over 100 women who survived out of 2,000.

Weissmann married American intelligence officer Kurt Klein, who liberated her and her fellow prisoners in Czechoslovakia. They then moved to the United States, where she became a citizen. Weissmann Klein published her autobiography, *All But My Life*, in 1957. It has become a classic work of literature, one that people read as a primary source of the Holocaust. She also became a powerful speaker and worked with many organizations to combat prejudice, teach tolerance, and promote education about the dangers of anti-Semitism. Gerda Weissmann Klein won the Presidential Medal of Freedom, the country's highest civilian award, in 2011 for her inspirational work.

The Soviets Advance

As prisoners marched west, Soviet forces approached Auschwitz, where thousands of prisoners remained, from the east. Most captives left behind had been too ill or weak to go on the death marches. In January 1945, members of the SS blew up the Auschwitz-Birkenau crematoria and gas chambers and destroyed documents and other evidence of their crimes. Then, many abandoned their posts in an effort to save themselves from the advancing Soviets.

Soviet soldiers of the First Ukrainian Front entered Auschwitz on January 27, 1945. The soldiers were shocked by the physical

Survivors leave Auschwitz in February 1945, after its liberation by Soviet forces.

state of most of the prisoners, giving chocolate bars to some. An American nurse later reported that the survivors' bodies were so thin that their skin tore easily. They had to be handled very carefully.

Ten-year-old Eva Mozes Kor ran "up to them [the soldiers] and they gave us hugs, cookies, and chocolates. Being so alone, a hug meant more than anybody could imagine, because that replaced the human worth we were starving for. We were not only starved for food but we were starved for human kindness."[3]

The Soviets found about 7,000 survivors at the Auschwitz camp complex. In Auschwitz's massive warehouses, soldiers recovered hundreds of thousands of men's suits, more than 800,000 pieces of women's clothing, and over 14,000 pounds (6,350 kilograms) of human hair. Still, the full measure of Nazi war crimes was yet to be revealed and understood.

German Leadership Breaks Down

Before the Soviets arrived, many Auschwitz survivors had been moved to another camp, Bergen-Belsen. The camp, with roughly

15,000 inmates at the end of 1944, became overcrowded with 60,000 by April 1945. The Nazis, unable or unwilling to accommodate their prisoners, abandoned them with little food or water and no way to escape. Those arriving from Auschwitz and other camps did not even have a place to sleep. The inmates languished in a nightmarish world. Bergen-Belsen was a different kind of horror-filled camp than Auschwitz had been. It seemed to some that their fellow prisoners were like skeletons shuffling around the camp. Then, on April 15, 1945, British tanks rolled into Bergen-Belsen, liberating the living dead.

What Bergen-Belsen's suffering prisoners did not know was that Himmler, the mastermind of the camps, freely gave up the camp to the Allied forces. Although Hitler ordered the camp destroyed, Himmler did not obey all his orders. Instead, he began making concessions to the enemy, allowing some Jews safe transportation to Switzerland for a fee and freeing others and sending them to Poland.

Himmler admitted to a colleague that, in hindsight, he would have acted differently and perhaps not have followed all of Hitler's policies. However, he maintained that obedience and discipline were paramount in building a strong country. His sentiments were echoed by many of his Third Reich colleagues after the war.

Alone in his private bunker in Berlin, Hitler realized that his dream of a united and victorious German empire, a reich he had bragged would last a thousand years, was finished. On April 20, 1945, the Soviets began bombing Berlin. Soon, they enclosed the entire city. The Germans were so desperate for soldiers that they included boys and old men in their ranks. As the Soviets made their way into Berlin, Hitler decided to end his own life rather than risk capture. He and his wife of one day, Eva Braun, died by suicide on April 30, 1945. In his final note, he blamed the Jews for causing the war.

Himmler's reaction to Germany's swift decline was different. During a final meeting at the Muerwick Navy School in northern Germany, he recommended that his SS commanders follow his lead and disappear into the countryside. His cowardice stunned Rudolf Höss, who had held him in great esteem.

HISTORY HAPPENED HERE: BERGEN-BELSEN CONCENTRATION CAMP

Bergen-Belsen, also called Belsen, was located near the villages of Bergen and Belsen in Germany. It was established in 1943 as a place for prisoners of war as well as a detention camp for Jews who would be exchanged for German prisoners of war. Its purpose shifted as the war waged on.

Originally designed for 10,000 prisoners, the camp's population swelled to six times that amount by the war's end. A lack of adequate food, water, and housing brought about the deaths of more than 35,000 people there between January and April 1945. Life in this camp had never been good for those forced to endure its horrors, but during those brutal months in early 1945, it became almost unsurvivable.

One such prisoner who did not survive Bergen-Belsen was Anne Frank, the young Jewish girl whose diary later served as a testament to life during the Holocaust. She died of typhus at this camp in March 1945, heartbreakingly close to the camp's liberation by the Allies.

Germany surrendered to the Allies on May 7, 1945. Two weeks later, Himmler was captured by British troops in Bremervörde, Germany. He wore an eyepatch as a disguise and identified himself as Heinrich Hitzinger. However, after taking him to an internment camp, the British forces soon realized whom they had in custody. Before army doctors could examine him on May 23, 1945, Himmler bit down on a cyanide capsule lodged in his teeth and killed himself.

Displaced

The Allied troops that liberated Auschwitz and other camps saw the horrific reality of the Nazi Final Solution: piles of bodies, ovens filled with ashes from corpses, and starving, disease-ridden men, women, and children. Now, the survivors had to piece their broken lives back together. Many survivors were uncertain they could return to countries such as Austria, Lithuania, Hungary, and Poland without fear of further anti-Semitism.

In Poland, such fears were warranted. Those who did return were victimized once again in violent pogroms. The worst occurred in 1946 in the village of Kielce, where unruly crowds murdered 42 Jews and injured 40 others.

Thousands of survivors tried moving west to France, Great Britain, and Belgium, among other nations. Temporary refugee centers were set up in places such as Bergen-Belsen, run by the newly formed United Nations Relief and Rehabilitation Administration. The armies of Great Britain, France, and the United States helped establish and maintain them.

Organizations such as the American Jewish Joint Distribution Committee supplied Holocaust survivors with clothing and food, while the Organization for Rehabilitation Through Training offered job training. Sh'erit ha-Pletah, or "Surviving Remnant," a group dedicated to helping people find homes around the world, worked to help Jews immigrate to other countries. However, options were limited.

The Jewish Brigade Group formed an organization to send displaced European Jews to Palestine in the Middle East. However, British authorities in control of the region did not allow the migration, in one instance turning back the ship *Exodus 1947* with 4,500 Holocaust survivors on board.

In December 1945, U.S. president Harry S. Truman eased restrictions on wartime immigrants, thus ushering in more than 41,000 people to the United States. Of these, 28,000 were Jews. Three years later, U.S. Congress passed the Displaced Persons Act, which subsequently brought 400,000 more refugees from Europe into the country. Other nations aided the effort, too, including New Zealand, Mexico, South Africa, Canada, and Australia.

Many Jewish leaders pushed for the creation of a Jewish homeland. In 1947, the UN General Assembly voted to partition the eastern Mediterranean region of Palestine into two states: one Jewish and the other Arab. Jewish leaders accepted this, while the Arabs of the region rejected it, leading to conflict that still exists today. Still, in 1948, the state of Israel was established. By 1953, at least

The Star of David, a long-established Jewish symbol, features prominently on the flag of Israel.

170,000 Jews had immigrated to what they considered their historic and spiritual homeland.

On Trial

In October 1943, foreign secretaries representing the Allied nations signed the Moscow Declaration. This pact stated that, at the war's end, those believed responsible for war crimes would be returned to those countries in which the crimes had been committed for judgment and punishment.

When the war ended, the wheels of justice began turning. World War II had taken the lives of at least 60 million people over 6 years. The Nazis' Final Solution had been responsible for killing at least 6 million Jews. About 1.5 million of them were children.

Between November 1945 and October 1946, one of the world's first war crime tribunals was held in Nuremberg, Germany. Its main defendant, Hermann Göring, as Hitler's second in command, had led the Third Reich's secret police known as the Gestapo. Göring sneered at the proceedings, but he and 23 others were charged with war crimes.

United States chief prosecutor Robert Jackson took leave from his position as associate justice of the United States Supreme Court

PAST MEETS PRESENT: HOLOCAUST DENIAL

Even in the face of photographs, documents, survivor testimonies, and other overwhelming evidence, some people claim even today that the Holocaust never happened. They allege that the concentration camps were created to house prisoners of war and that the gas chambers were fictional. Some cannot believe a government would go to such lengths to murder people. Others deny it happened because they are anti-Semitic and think the Holocaust is a story invented by Jews to make Germans and other eastern Europeans look bad.

David Irving, a self-proclaimed historian who published several books claiming that the Holocaust was a hoax, received condemnation for his denial of the Holocaust. When a scholar named Deborah E. Lipstadt criticized him and his research in the early 1990s, he tried to sue her. However, the judge ruled against him, agreeing with Lipstadt's assessment.

Cambridge professor Richard J. Evans, after much study, wrote of Irving's work: "Not one of [Irving's] books ... can be taken on trust as an accurate representation of its historical subject. All of them are completely worthless as history ... if we mean by historian someone who is concerned to discover the truth about the past ... Irving is not a historian."[1] Holocaust deniers twist facts and ignore a vast amount of evidence to support their claim that this very real, very tragic event was a lie.

1. Richard J. Evans, "Evans: David Irving, Hitler and Holocaust Denial," in Holocaust Denial on Trial, Emory University, www.hdot.org/evans/# (accessed January 19, 2021).

to take part in the trials. Jackson's burden of proof was not very high; the defendants were hated and their conviction was expected. Jackson also had plenty of evidence: The Nazis kept meticulous records of deportations and methods of destruction. Nevertheless, tying specific Third Reich officials to particular crimes proved tricky, so instead, Jackson attempted to prove premeditation and prejudice

This photograph was taken on the third day of the Nuremberg trials.

against the Jews. He also intended to directly link Göring to their destruction. However, the arrogant Gestapo leader did not budge, simply claiming that the trials were part of the spoils of war: The victors take revenge on the defeated.

The trials dragged on for nearly one year, at times tedious, at other times tense. Jackson and his fellow prosecutors built their case, piece by piece. One of the more powerful moments occurred when film footage taken at the death camps was shown in court. It was the first time that the media and the public were given a glimpse at the horror of the Holocaust.

Göring remained calm and collected. On the day he took the witness stand, it appeared that his demeanor and his unwillingness to cooperate might save him. As 500 spectators watched, Göring and Jackson battled for the upper hand. Göring claimed that the actions he took during the war were simply to protect his country. He presented himself as a patriotic German, sacrificing himself for the good of his homeland.

However, five days into Göring's testimony, the sharp-minded Jackson tried a different approach. Göring—under intense questioning—admitted his part in the Final Solution. The fate of Göring and 10 other defendants was soon sealed. The verdict: guilty. The punishment: hanging.

Göring killed himself by biting a cyanide capsule two hours before his death sentence was to be carried out. The poison had been hidden in his cell the entire time. In this final decision of his life, Göring took a liberty he had helped deny to so many.

Unlike Göring, one high-profile war criminal escaped justice. Auschwitz's "Angel of Death," Josef Mengele, remained a fugitive long after World War II ended. His twisted brand of medicine accounts for some of the worst atrocities committed during World War II. In 1949, after keeping a low profile in Europe, Mengele fled to Argentina. There, he made a living carrying out illegal abortions and eventually buying a large share of a pharmaceutical company. He later went into hiding, and with the help of family and friends, eluded justice. After an exhaustive investigation, authorities discovered Mengele's remains in 1985, six years after his death.

Answering for Auschwitz

Rudolf Höss, the quiet and deliberate commandant of Auschwitz, initially escaped from authorities. As the Soviet Red Army moved on the death camp, Höss fled into Germany and lived under the assumed name of Franz Lang. In 1946, he was discovered by Allied military police and handed over to Polish officials. His trial began in Warsaw, Poland, on March 11, 1947. The auditorium in which it was held was packed with journalists and Auschwitz survivors.

Like so many of his fellow Nazis, Höss said that he simply followed the orders given to him. Therefore, according to him, he was not responsible for the suffering and death of so many. When he took the stand at his trial, his interpreter, Joseph Maier, said he had no emotion, no sign of nervousness or fear. His deposition at the trial recounted in some detail the Third Reich's greatest crimes. He denied little but wrote that he sometimes felt uncomfortable sending children to the gas chambers: "Adolf Eichmann … explained to me that it was especially the children who have to be killed first, because where was the logic in killing a generation of older people and leaving alive a generation of young people who can be possible avengers of their parents and can constitute a new biological cell for the reemerging of this people."[4]

Höss was sentenced to death in 1947 and taken to Auschwitz. Former inmates had asked the court to carry out the sentence on the grounds of the death camp. The court agreed. At dawn on April 16,

German POWs built the gallows. Höss spent his last hours in the former Block 11, which had been known as the Death Block.

At 10 a.m., his hands cuffed behind his back, Rudolf Höss walked one last time down the camp's main street toward the gallows. A noose awaited him. He could see the prisoner barracks, the gas chambers, and the crematoria. At 10:08 a.m., as a priest recited the last rites, a hangman kicked a stool from beneath Höss, his feet popped the trap door, and his legs swung free. He was pronounced dead at 10:21. He was Auschwitz's last fatality.

Looking Back and Into the Future

On January 27, 2020, more than 100 survivors of the Auschwitz complex gathered at the place that is now called Auschwitz-Birkenau Memorial and Museum. They assembled to commemorate the 75th anniversary of Auschwitz's liberation. As the survivors enter old age, it becomes paramount to remember their ordeal. Increasingly, many feel they must speak out because they are afraid of the Holocaust happening again in some form.

Naftali Fürst was just a boy when he endured the horrors of Auschwitz and then Buchenwald concentration camp. He did not begin talking about his experiences until 2005. It became clear to him that he had to. "I think it [the Holocaust] can happen again," he said. "It wasn't a different planet. Humans did that … I have a duty to tell [my story]." He feels compelled to speak out because people believe "that it didn't happen."[5]

Fürst's fear that another Holocaust-like event could happen is not unwarranted. Following the war, the United Nations passed Resolution 96-I, which made genocide punishable under international law. More than 130 nations have agreed to it. Yet this resolution has not halted the hatred and violence against groups of people that lead to genocide. In fact, there have been other instances of genocide in the decades since World War II.

Many point to the actions of the Cambodian government in the 1970s as an example of genocide. It systematically killed 1.7 million people over four years, targeting the educated, whom they deemed as being "tainted" by Western culture, as well as Christians, Buddhists, and Muslims.

FROM THE SOURCE: A LETTER FROM RUDOLF HÖSS TO HIS CHILDREN

Five days before his execution, Höss wrote a letter to his children. The commanding officer of Auschwitz, who had shown no emotion or evidence of moral struggle about his part of the Holocaust, showed a different side to his family. His message to his children gave them advice:

> *Your daddy has to leave you now ... The biggest mistake of my life was that I believed everything faithfully which came from the top, and I didn't dare to have the least bit of doubt about the truth of that which was presented to me. Walk through life with your eyes open ... Don't just let your mind speak, but listen above all to the voice in your heart ... Have ... soft and feeling hearts. Retain these throughout your later life. This is the most important thing. Only later will you understand that and will you remember my last words.*[1]

While Höss showed regret in these messages, he did not seem to—or perhaps could not—comprehend what he had done in the name of duty to the Third Reich.

1. Quoted in John W. Primomo, *Architect of Death at Auschwitz: A Biography of Rudolf Hoss* (Jefferson, NC: McFarland & Company, 2020), pp. 190–191.

In 1994, in the African country of Rwanda, ethnic tensions boiled over after the death of the nation's president. Extremist Hutus massacred more than 800,000 Tutsis and moderate Hutus. Much of the killing was committed by regular citizens, who were encouraged to murder their neighbors and even relatives.

In 2021, the United States declared that the Chinese government was committing genocide against hundreds of thousands of Uighurs and other predominantly Muslim ethnic minorities by forcing them into internment camps, mandating sterilizations,

People of all backgrounds and ages visit Auschwitz-Birkenau to honor the memories of those who suffered and died there.

and separating their families. The United States asserted that these were efforts to destroy their culture and indoctrinate loyalty to the Chinese government.

Clearly, genocide and the motivations to commit it still exist. More needs to be done to educate people about racism and discrimination. As the United States Holocaust Memorial Museum explained, "It's important to remember that the Holocaust did not start from gas chambers & murder. The hatred slowly developed from ideas, words, stereotypes & prejudice, through legal exclusion, escalating violence & dehumanization."[6] Education can halt the development of such blind hatred and injustice.

To combat future Holocausts, nations around the world will need to cooperate to prevent such atrocities and swiftly intervene when necessary. To honor the victims of Auschwitz and the Holocaust, we must not only learn about the past but promise action in the future.

How You See History

1. What might be the best way to educate people about the Holocaust?
2. Why might people deny the Holocaust took place in the face of so much evidence?
3. Why do you think genocide is still a danger today?

TIMELINE

1933

Adolf Hitler becomes chancellor of Germany on January 30. The first Nazi concentration camp, Dachau, is opened near Munich.

1938

On November 9 and 10, hundreds of Jewish businesses and synagogues are targeted in an attack known as Kristallnacht, or the Night of Broken Glass.

1939

Germany invades Poland in early September, beginning World War II.

1940

In April, in the Polish village of Oświęcim, the construction of a new concentration camp begins, built from deserted army barracks.

June 1941

In June, Germany invades the Soviet Union. Special Nazi death squads, known as Einsatzgruppen, incite pogroms against Jews.

Fall 1941

In September, the first group of prisoners is killed in a gas chamber at Auschwitz. Beginning in October, prisoners build an extension to Auschwitz, known as Auschwitz-Birkenau.

December 1941

On December 7, Japanese warplanes attack Pearl Harbor, Hawaii. The United States joins the war.

1942

At the Wannsee Conference, Nazi officials organize the "Final Solution to the Jewish Question." Anne Frank, her family, and four friends go into hiding in the Netherlands. In the United States, the internment of Japanese Americans begins.

1943

In May, Josef Mengele becomes the head physician at the Auschwitz camp complex.

June 1944

Allied forces invade Normandy, France, on D-Day, June 6.

October 1944

Some Sonderkommandos working at Auschwitz revolt but are soon deterred and executed by the Nazis.

January 1945

On January 27, the Soviet army liberates Auschwitz-Birkenau and its remaining 7,000 survivors.

April 1945

Hitler dies by suicide in his bunker on April 30 as the Soviets attack Berlin.

May 1945

German armed forces surrender in the west on May 7 and in the east on May 9.

September 1945

Japan formally surrenders on September 2, ending World War II.

November 1945

The Nuremberg trials begin.

1947

Rudolf Höss is executed at Auschwitz on April 16; the former commandant of the camp is the last person to die there.

NOTES

Introduction: Why We Must Remember

1. Quoted in "Anti-Semitism in the US," ADL, www.adl.org/what-we-do/anti-semitism/anti-semitism-in-the-us (accessed June 10, 2020).

Chapter One: The Road to War

1. "Deceiving the Public," United States Holocaust Memorial Museum, www.ushmm.org/wlc/en/article.php?ModuleId=10007822 (accessed June 11, 2020).
2. Quoted in Jeffrey Herf, *The Jewish Enemy: Nazi Propaganda During World War II and the Holocaust* (Cambridge, MA: Belknap Press of Harvard University Press, 2006), p. 23.
3. Quoted in Christa Kamenetsky, *Children's Literature in Hitler's Germany: The Cultural Policy of National Socialism* (Athens, OH: Ohio University Press, 2019), e-book.
4. Quoted in Jonathan Kirsch, *The Short, Strange Life of Herschel Grynszpan* (New York, NY: Liveright Publishing Corporation, 2013), p. 153.
5. Quoted in Rita Thalmann and Emmanuel Feinermann, *Crystal Night: 9-10 November 1938* (New York, NY: Holocaust Library, 1974), p. 11.
6. "William (Welek) Luksenburg Describes the First Night of the German Invasion of Poland," United States Holocaust Memorial Museum, encyclopedia.ushmm.org/content/en/oral-history/william-welek-luksenburg (accessed January 6, 2021).
7. Quoted in Andrew Rawson, *Auschwitz: The Nazi Solution* (South Yorkshire, UK: Pen and Sword Military, 2015), p. 5.

Chapter Two: Violence and Terror

1. Quoted in Eleanor H. Ayer, *In the Ghettos: Teens Who Survived the Ghettos of the Holocaust* (New York, NY: Rosen Publishing, 1999), p. 24.
2. Saul Friedländer, *The Years of Extermination: Nazi Germany and the Jews, 1939–1945* (New York: HarperCollins, 2007), p. 92.
3. Daniel Jonah Goldhagen, *Hitler's Willing Executioners: Ordinary Germans and the Holocaust* (New York: Vintage Books, 1997), p. 149.

4. Quoted in Laurence Rees, *Auschwitz: A New History* (New York, NY: PublicAffairs), p. 8.

5. Rees, *Auschwitz: A New History*, p. 79.

Chapter Three: Living and Dying in Auschwitz

1. Quoted in Ruth Kluger, *Still Alive: A Holocaust Girlhood Remembered* (New York, NY: The Feminist Press at The City University of New York, 2001), pp. 91-92.

2. Cecilie Klein-Pollack, "Cecilie Klein-Pollack Describes Arrival at Auschwitz," United States Holocaust Memorial Museum, encyclopedia.ushmm.org/content/en/oral-history/cecilie-klein-pollack-describes-arrival-at-auschwitz (accessed January 12, 2021).

3. Quoted in "Factories of Death," *Auschwitz: Inside the Nazi State, 2004–2005*, PBS, www.pbs.org/auschwitz/about/transcripts_3.html (accessed January 12, 2021).

4. Gretchen Engle Schafft, *From Racism to Genocide: Anthropology in the Third Reich* (Champaign, IL: University of Illinois Press, 2004), p. 172.

5. Quoted in Laurence Rees, *Auschwitz: A New History* (New York, NY: PublicAffairs), p. 170.

Chapter Four: The Survivors

1. Tom Parry, "Henia Bryer Survived Four Nazi Camps and a Meeting with Dr Death: Courageous Teenager Who Never Gave In," *The Mirror*, January 25, 2013, www.mirror.co.uk/news/real-life-stories/henia-bryer-survived-four-nazi-1556662.

2. Quoted in Primo Levi, *Survival at Auschwitz* (Hawthorne, CA: BN Publishing, 2008), p. 39.

3. Quoted in Debórah Dwork and Robert Jan van Pelt, *Holocaust: A History* (New York, NY: W.W. Norton, 2002), p. 367.

4. Laurence Rees, *Auschwitz: A New History* (New York, NY: PublicAffairs), p. 175.

5. Quoted in Rees, *Auschwitz: A New History*, pp. 144–145.

Chapter Five: Liberation

1. Quoted in "What Did the World Know?" Facing History and Ourselves, www.facinghistory.org/holocaust-and-human-behavior/chapter-9/what-did-world-know (accessed January 26, 2021).

2. Benjamin Ferencz, "Benjamin (Beryl) Ferencz Describes Collecting Evidence of Death Marches," United States Holocaust Memorial Museum, encyclopedia.ushmm.org/content/en/oral-history/benjamin-beryl-ferencz-describes-collecting-evidence-of-death-marches (accessed January 19, 2021).
3. Quoted in "Auschwitz: Inside the Nazi State," PBS, accessed www.pbs.org/auschwitz/40-45/liberation/ (accessed January 19, 2021).
4. Quoted in "Rudolf Höss," Jewish Virtual Library, www.jewishvirtuallibrary.org/jsource/biography/Hoess.html (accessed January 26, 2021).
5. Quoted in "'I think it can happen again' — Holocaust survivor meets Merkel ahead of Auschwitz liberation anniversary," DW, www.dw.com/en/i-think-it-can-happen-again-holocaust-survivor-meets-merkel-ahead-of-auschwitz-liberation-anniversary/a-52097360 (accessed January 26, 2021).
6. @AuschwitzMuseum, "When we look at Auschwitz we see the end of the process. It's important to remember that the Holocaust actually did not start from gas chambers. This hatred gradually developed from words, stereotypes & prejudice through legal exclusion, dehumanisation & escalating violence," Twitter, November 26, 2018, twitter.com/auschwitzmuseum/status/1067175336184606720?lang=en.

FOR MORE INFORMATION

Books: Nonfiction

Bornstein, Michael. *Survivors Club: The True Story of a Very Young Prisoner of Auschwitz*. New York, NY: Square Fish, 2019.

Croy, Anita. *Anne Frank*. New York, NY: Lucent Press, 2020.

Rees, Laurence. *The Holocaust: A New History*. New York, NY: PublicAffairs, 2018.

Books: Fiction

Adlington, L. J. *The Red Ribbon*. London, UK: Hot Key Books, 2018.

Kraus, Otto B. *The Children's Block: A Novel Based on the True Story of an Auschwitz Survivor*. New York, NY: Pegasus Books, 2020.

Levitin, Sonia. *Journey to America: Escaping the Holocaust to Freedom*. New York, NY: Aladdin, 2020.

Websites

Auschwitz-Birkenau Memorial and Museum

auschwitz.org/en/

The grounds of the infamous camp complex serve as a monument to the dead, educating about the Holocaust and allowing people to walk the same place where more than 1 million prisoners lost their lives.

Oral History with Dina Babbitt

collections.ushmm.org/search/catalog/irn37287

Watch and listen as Dina Babbitt tells of her time at Auschwitz painting portraits of her fellow prisoners.

United States Holocaust Memorial Museum

www.ushmm.org

Called a living memorial, the museum is tasked with teaching people about the events of the Holocaust, promoting human dignity, and reminding us what prejudice and hatred can lead to.

INDEX

PHOTO CREDITS

Cover Imagno/Contributor/Hulton Archive/Getty Images; p. 4 Krysja/Shutterstock.com; p. 7 Everett Collection/Shutterstock.com; pp. 9, 20, 69 ullstein bild/Contributor/ullstein bild/Getty Images; pp. 12, 30 Bettmann/Contributor/Bettmann/Getty Images; p. 16 Auckland War Memorial Museum/File:Treaty of Versailles, English version.jpg/Wikimedia Commons/PD; p. 18 Sean Gallup/Staff/Getty Images News/Getty Images; pp. 23, 44, 60 ullstein bild Dtl./Contributor/ullstein bild/Getty Images; p. 24 Library of Congress/Contributor/Corbis Historical/Getty Images; p. 26 Keystone/Stringer/Hulton Archive/Getty Images; p. 27 Universal History Archive/Contributor/Universal Images Group/Getty Images; pp. 33, 78 Keystone-France/Contributor/Gamma-Keystone/Getty Images; pp. 37, 48, 58 picture alliance/Contributor/picture alliance/Getty Images; p. 38 Hulton Archive/Staff/Hulton Archive/Getty Images; p. 41 SOPA Images/Contributor/LightRocket/Getty Images; p. 45 Laski Diffusion/Contributor/Hulton Archive/Getty Images; pp. 47, 82 Galerie Bilderwelt/Contributor/Hulton Archive/Getty Images; p. 50 Dna-Dennis/File:WW2-Holocaust-Europe.png/Wikimedia Commons/CC BY 3-0; p. 51 MirSiwy/Shutterstock.com; p. 53 JANEK SKARZYNSKI/Staff/AFP/Getty Images; p. 55 H. Miller/Stringer/Hulton Archive/Getty Images; p. 62 Francois LOCHON/Contributor/Gamma-Rapho/Getty Images; p. 64 Natalia Fedosenko/Contributor/TASS/Getty Images; p. 66 WOJTEK RADWANSKI/Contributor/AFP/Getty Images; p. 68 ERIC SCHWAB/Staff/AFP/Getty Images; p. 70 Image Bank/Alamy Stock Photo; p. 75 Richard Blanshard/Contributor/Hulton Archive/Getty Images; p. 86 Atlantide Phototravel/Corbis Documentary/Getty Images; p. 88 Ralph Morse/Contributor/The LIFE Picture Collection/Getty Images; p. 92 NurPhoto/Contributor/NurPhoto/Getty Images.

ABOUT THE AUTHOR

Therese Harasymiw has written and edited over 350 nonfiction books for children and teens, including works on Anne Frank and World War II. Harasymiw received an English degree from Providence College and a master of education degree in English education from the State University of New York at Buffalo. A former high school literature teacher, she works as an editor in educational publishing. Harasymiw and her family reside in Rochester, New York.